From the Hart

Two Decades of Columns, Kindness, and Kitchen-Table Wisdom

JANET HART LEONARD

Janet Hart Leonard's gift is not writing, though she is very skilled at that. Janet is a storyteller. She pulls readers in with personal moments and challenges us to see with kinder eyes and live with more open hearts. Her faith-grounded stories remind us that we can choose to be better people. She makes us laugh. She makes us cry. She makes us think. I cannot count the people who have told me that her column, "From the Hart," is the first thing they read when the Monday edition arrives. Thanks for making us all feel like old friends visiting your Little House on the Alley.

STU CLAMPITT, Publisher
Hamilton County Reporter Newspaper

If you've ever had the pleasure of a Janet-hug, her words have the same effect. Her wisdom has marinated for decades, and she offers it with sincerity and grace that wrap you up and let you breathe. Just like the kind of hug you never want to end. You'll catch the scent of Jesus as you read because weathered faith lingers like that.

TWYLA FRANZ, Daughters First Retreat Leadership Team Member,
Writer

These short stories cover the full breadth of the human experience: identity, purpose, loss, and faith. Janet approaches life's greatest challenges with experienced wisdom and surprising peace, inviting us to examine our own circumstances and struggles with hopeful contemplation. Delivered with the warmth of a summer morning on the back porch, her words fall softly and encourage us to embrace the world around us with grace.

ERIN GRENEAUX, award-winning author of
Sunday God Meets Monday Mom and
the Gold Feather Gardeners series

A truly heartwarming book that immediately connects the reader to the author's stories. The scripture and questions help promote reflection on your own personal journey. A book you will read more than once.

MARIANNE JACOBI, Janet's fourth-grade teacher at
First Ward Elementary School, Noblesville, Indiana, 1965–66

Janet Hart Leonard writes with the kind of wisdom that only comes from living fully, falling down, and getting back up with faith. Her personal stories draw you in immediately, and before you know it, you're looking back at your own life with new eyes. She reminds us that we're never too old, it's never too late, and God has a plan for every detail of our journey. Peppered with scripture insight and just the right dash of humor, this book is a balm for the weary soul. I highly recommend it to every reader.

AMANDA SCHAEFER, award-winning author of
Holy Plot Twists: God Is Still Writing Your Story
and host of the podcast *A Cup of Gratitude*

As Janet's publisher, I've had the privilege of reading every word in this book, multiple times. Each time, I discover something that ministers to my heart in new ways. Janet writes with authenticity, grace, and a tender honesty that makes you feel like you're sitting with a trusted friend. Her stories don't just tell you about faith; they show you what it looks like to walk it out in real life, through valleys and detours, heartbreak and joy. Her wisdom is timeless, the kind both younger readers and those of us with a few more miles on our hearts desperately need. This is a book I'm honored to bring into the world.

ANDREA LENDE, Publisher, Beatitudes Publishing

Dictionary definitions sourced from Merriam-Webster Dictionary (merriam-webster.com) and Google Dictionary, with some definitions adapted by the author.

Some stories in this book originally appeared in the author's column in the Hamilton County Reporter between 2020 and 2026. Excerpts are used with permission by the owners, Stuart Clampitt, Ray Adler, Isaac Taylor, and Paul Poteet.

It Takes a Village by Emily Catron Alexander originally appeared in the Hamilton County Reporter, May 2025. Used with permission.

The Let Them Theory by Mel Robbins is referenced with appreciation.

www.janethartleonard.com

Interior & Cover Design Ruth Hovsepian
Author Photo Matt Doudt

Paperback ISBN: 978-1-962581-86-8
Hardcover SBN: 978-1-962581-87-5
eBook ISBN: 978-1-962581-88-2

BEATITUDES PUBLISHING

This book is dedicated to my husband, Chuck,

who taught me that the best love story

can be written in the winter of your life.

Contents

Foreword IX

A Note from Janet XI

Before We Begin 1

Vintage Wisdom 5

1. Finding Wisdom 7

2. Dear Younger Janet 10

3. When I'm Overwhelmed 14

4. The Power of a Gentle Voice 19

5. From Let Them to Let Me Let Them 22

6. The Power of Five 28

7. The Power of Ponderings 33

8. Lead Me Not to be a Fixer 37

9. Declining the Invitation 41

10. The Power of Words 45

11. Finding Joy in the Quiet 48

12. Don't Be Ugly   51

Meandering Thoughts   53

13. Starting Something New   55

14. Meandering Thoughts   59

15. Finding Heavenly Peace   63

16. Even if...   67

17. The Affirmations   71

18. When God Gives You a Dream   75

19. Sustaining Grace   79

20. But I Have the Right to be Angry   83

21. Empty-Heart Syndrome   87

22. It Takes a Village   91

23. Could I Have This Dance   94

24. She   97

My Final Thoughts... for now   100

Janet's Southern Comfort Recipes   103

Foreword

In June 2022, my wife launched her first book, *When the Hart Speaks*, surrounded by friends and family at Ginger's Café, where everyone knows her name.

As HOTA (Husband of the Author), I was asked to make a few remarks. I remember saying that when a person is passionate about a task, it shows. Janet is passionate about her writing—whether it's her weekly newspaper column or a book.

Following its publication, there were numerous opportunities for book signings and speaking engagements with book clubs and women's groups. All the while, a second book simmered in her mind. Nothing seemed to come together, and still she wrote.

Then came the Snowmageddon of 2026, and Janet found inspiration in being snowed in with ten inches of snow and temperatures below zero, wearing "writing pajamas." In the morning, she was at our kitchen table by 5:00, having changed out of her sleeping pajamas, drinking her coffee, and tapping away at the keyboard. She said the "voices" would wake her and tell her it was time to put ink to paper or fingers to keys. By Saturday,

January 31st, just a week after the snow began to fall, *From the Hart* was finished.

As I read the rough draft, these words came to my mind: faith-based, positive, and uplifting.

Let the reading begin.

Chuck Leonard and Janet have been married since February 23, 2014. He served as the Hamilton Southeastern School Superintendent in Fishers, Indiana, from 1984 to 2001. He was the official scoreboard keeper for the Colts Football Team from 1984 to 2024, never missing a home game. Weather permitting, he can be found on the golf course several days a week, trying to score his third hole-in-one.

A Note from Janet

"Write softly and do not carry a big stick." —JHL

Does that sound like a twist on a quote we have all heard before? Sorry, Teddy Roosevelt.

Whenever I write, I try my best not to use words or thoughts that will harm my readers. They hear enough words every day that hurt their hearts, crush their dreams, and ruffle their feathers.

Soft words invite my readers into a world where kindness matters and hearts are hugged. Harsh words, those that carry a big stick, sow discord and cause hearts to ache.

May these words of my mouth and this meditation of my heart be pleasing in your sight, Lord, my Rock and my Redeemer. (Psalm 19:14)

I pray the same over the words I write. I've often said I want the epitaph on my gravestone to read, "Her words mattered."

I often meander in my writing, not knowing where my thoughts are going. Some days, I write for the pure joy of telling stories and writing down my thoughts. Destination unknown.

As I begin to put my thoughts together for this book, I'm sitting at my kitchen table, enjoying the flickering of a burning candle while devouring a few store-bought peanut butter no-bake cookies, my current obsession. A bit of snow is on its way here. I'm wearing my favorite comfy slippers, and the bedclothes are in the dryer. Did anyone else have a mother who called the sheets "bedclothes?" For me, that's an endearing phrase.

Did you know a person who loves words is called a logophile? Any other logophiles out there? When I hear or read a new word, I write it down along with its meaning unless it's a word I don't like, meaning it feels harsh or clumsy. I save words to use in my columns and books.

I have written a newspaper column, "From the Hart," for almost twenty years. Did you know that a newspaper columnist is sometimes called an ink-stained wretch? It refers to a writer devoted to their craft, marked by ink. Back in the day, a writer's fingers were stained by ink from using quill pens. I think a modern-day writer could be called a keyboard warrior.

The pressure of writing a second book is real. I fear it will go from a TBR (To Be Read) to a DNF (Did Not Finish). I fear my words will not make a difference.

One of the most challenging aspects of writing is rejection. I remember getting my first rejection email. Hundreds of writers submitted their work to a very popular Christian community. I took that rejected piece and turned it into a column that received many positive comments. The thing about writers is that we tend to take rejection personally (like, who doesn't?). We hear, "You're not good enough" or "You'll never be like so-and-so." Oh, the daggers of rejection and comparison are real.

I will continue to write soft words and not carry a big stick. Big sticks poke and prod, and can do significant harm. I hope my words offer my readers a soft place to land. I hope my words encourage hearts that are weary and worn by life's challenges. I hope my words help others see the goodness of God in a world that sometimes challenges their Faith.

As I write this book, I have entered my seventh decade. In the pages you will read, I hope, there is some wisdom that will make your journey through life a bit easier. I've stubbed my heart on the wrong decisions, gotten lost on the detours, and learned lessons the brutally hard way. May you learn from my mistakes and realize that yours are not fatal. I pray your heart is hugged and your Faith deepened as you read my words.

My thoughts don't always have a destination, but they will forever be written from my heart. I hope your mind and your heart enjoy the meandering of my thoughts and find encouragement along the way.

Janet Hart Leonard

From the Hart

Before We Begin

While writing this book, my mind kept changing lanes, so to speak. I had meandering thoughts about the wisdom I've gathered over my seventy years. As I wrote, I kept thinking I was writing two books, so I did what a writer does who doesn't want to write two books—I put them together into one. Maybe I'm wiser than I think I am.

"If I have knowledge but lack wisdom, I am like a cowbell. I make noise, but no one wants to listen." —JHL

That thought might sound a little like 1 Corinthians 13:1: "If I speak in the tongues of men and of angels, but have not love, I am only a resounding gong or a clanging cymbal."

I pray I never come across as an educated idiot or full of pompous poo. I hope to share the wisdom I've found after discovering so much that is unwise.

So how do I define wisdom?

It's like a recipe. Gather knowledge. Throw in a few bad decisions. Apply the facts generously to the mix. Drop in some sweet thoughts. Throw in a few more bad decisions. Stir briskly for a good while. Let rest. Generously grease a baking pan with butter. (Butter is added to every recipe I make... well, pretty much.) Whip together all the ingredients and pour into a pan filled with hard knocks. Bake for seventy years and serve to all who will listen.

I think you get the gist of what I am trying to say.

We go to school to gather facts and knowledge. Then we live our lives, learning to navigate detours, hitting a few bumps in the road, and chasing away more than a few evil wolves and dastardly skunks. We end up where we are supposed to be. It may not look as we expected, but if we learn to appreciate the new colors and beauty of the landscape, we will have found wisdom.

Merriam-Webster defines wisdom as the ability to discern inner qualities and relationships, good sense, and accumulated scientific knowledge.

My definition has nothing to do with anything scientific. It's more about math—adding up all that has led up to being seventy years young.

One of my favorite books in the Old Testament is Proverbs. It offers insight into applying wisdom in practical ways so we can live a good life, not just for ourselves but also for others. Proverbs offers a holy blend of common sense and lessons to learn. I've been known to say that it points us in the right direction, but the Holy Spirit nudges us and sometimes shoves us.

Proverbs was written by Solomon, who is said to be the wisest man who ever lived. We need his wisdom with us today. I could go down a deep, dark, scary rabbit hole about the trials and tribulations of today's world, but that's not what this book is about. It's about wisdom and finding hope. It's about the value of kindness and doing the right thing, even when it's not the easy thing.

I pray that you will hear the words from my heart. As I sit here at my kitchen table (where I do most of my writing), I am writing the words I would say if you were sitting across from me, sharing thoughts and a cup of coffee or tea, whichever you prefer.

So, without further ado, I bring you *From the Hart*.

Vintage Wisdom

Finding Wisdom

A not-so-funny thing happened on the way to seventy—I discovered wisdom. I would love to have found it before then, but that's not how it works. I gathered it along the way. I found hard rocks—life's hard rocks—that had hit me. I picked them up and have carried them with me over the years.

For some reason, I remember the song I heard as a little girl, "Pickin' up paw paws, put 'em in your pocket." The thing is, I heard "Pickin' up nuggets, put 'em in your pocket." Those are wisdom nuggets. It's a good thing I have deep pockets. In this book, I will share my nuggets.

(BTW, paw paws are from the Pawpaw Tree. Imagine a green potato hanging from a tree. In my opinion, they are beautifully ugly.)

How many times have I said, "If only I knew then what I know now?" Perhaps you have said the same thing.

I am writing this book to help others avoid anxiety, hurt, discouragement, a broken heart, frustration, heartache, mental anguish, physical exhaustion, and the feeling of being overwhelmed by life. I mentioned heart issues more than once. That's because I think it's the most tender part of our being and the one with the most issues. That's the opinion of someone who has never had a heart attack but has had her heart attacked and broken more than a few times.

Hard knocks lead to clarity in how we see others. We gain a clearer vision as we begin to see people for who they are. We can more easily recognize a wolf in sheep's clothing.

Detours help us realize that we are more resilient and adaptable than we ever thought. What was once thought to be impossible to do, we do it and do it well. Insert a well-placed "Hallelujah!"

Taking everything personally for so many years wore me to a frazzle.

Frazzle: to put into a state of nervous fatigue.

Perhaps you can relate.

The book of Proverbs has thirty-one chapters—one for each day of the month. What if I dared you to read one chapter a day and journal in a notebook what you learned? Would you take the dare?

What if you made a list of all the wisdom you gained over the years? What if you wrote those lessons in a journal to pass on to your children and grandchildren?

Legacy: What you leave your children and grandchildren after you are no longer—the example you set and the story you lived. Your legacy doesn't just tell others what you did, but why you did it.

What if the things you've been through could guide them to live a life of perseverance and determination? What if you could help them avoid the same mistakes you made? What if you could help others live an easier life?

What if you could show others how to live each day with new insight, helping them navigate their days more easily and stay focused on their goals?

These were my thoughts as I put this book together. Now grab a cup of coffee or tea, cozy up in a warm comforter, and sit back as you ponder and continue to read my thoughts.

***

What do you wish you had known when you were younger?

Who had the greatest influence on your decisions?

What legacy do you hope to leave your children and grandchildren?

Dear Younger Janet

It's 1974, and you just graduated from Noblesville High School. Oh, do I have things to tell you! Some things you won't appreciate until much later. You will someday find yourself saying, "If only I had known then what I know now."

In the years to come, you will be taught lessons you never wanted to learn. Your mistakes will be your best teachers. You will sometimes think you earned a bachelor's degree in regrets. You will be surprised to see that others will benefit from the lessons you learn the hard way.

You will encounter many detours in your life. Those detours will take you to places you never imagined. Some will be scary. Be brave, and you will find you are right where you belong. (Even at a car dealership)

While you are busy designing your life, it will become tangled and appear messy. Just wait until you see its new design.

You will travel through valleys where you will see the shadow of death. Fear not, for you will see that your greatest joys lie just beyond the shadows.

Some mornings, you will wake up wanting to pull the covers over your head. Get up and move. Don't pitch a tent in your sadness or frustration.

It's okay to recognize your pain for what it is. It's okay to admit you're not in a good place. Go for a walk. Clean out a closet. Scrub a toilet. It will get better. Trust me on this.

There will be chapters in your life you won't like, but they will inspire others. Allow God to hold your pen as He writes your story. Your Faith will grow stronger in your weakest moments. Hold fast to your Faith, for it will be your anchor in every storm you face. Always keep your Bible close by and read it regularly. (I know you won't read it daily.)

It's okay to have doubts and questions. It's okay to tell God you are angry with Him. He already knows it. It's during those moments when you are having honest conversations with God that He will reveal Himself and demonstrate who He is in your life.

> Commit to the Lord whatever you do, and he will establish your plans. (Proverbs 16:3)

People will disappoint you. It's a fact of life. Over time, you will learn to trust the right people, but there will always be that one who sneaks into your life for a short time. You will look back and say, "Lesson learned." You will find beauty in watching someone walk away. You will call it "The beauty of the backside."

You will make decisions and later think, "What was I thinking?" This will involve relationships, fashion, home décor, and hairstyles. You will love big hair and shoulder pads. The mauve floral sofa will be beautiful until it isn't.

There will be times when you will make excuses for others' bad behavior. You will tell yourself things will get better. You will rationalize others' conduct as acceptable. You will be wrong. *Girl, you deserve better.*

Each bad decision, bad relationship, and bad choice is simply the process of refining and shaping you into the woman you are meant to be. The refining is hard and hurts. You will wish the refining would make you skinny. It won't.

On occasion, you will say, "Life isn't supposed to be this way." You will keep the Ten Commandments and the fifty-two rules of your church, thinking this will guarantee you an easy life with things going as you planned. You will be wrong.

Life will be like trying to wrangle yourself into a sports bra. You wrangle and you sweat, eventually getting things where they should be, but you will be worn out.

While you listen to your heart, listen to what your mind is telling you, and pay even closer attention to what your gut says. You will learn to trust your gut more than your heart. Your heart will wrap you in emotions. Your mind will rationalize and justify actions. Your gut will proclaim the truth you need to embrace. Value the opinion of your gut.

You will have a wonderful circle of friends. You will dance and forever sing the songs of the 70s. You will have a great therapist. You will need him many times over the years. It's okay to have one.

You will do many things with fear and trepidation. You will get used to wearing your big girl panties. Your smile will hide your fears. People will have no idea how scared you are.

Being alone and feeling unloved for fourteen years will be one of your greatest challenges. Your prince charming will someday sit catty-corner from you at the kitchen table. Together, while sipping your morning coffee, you will watch the birds at the feeders. This will be one of your greatest joys. And you will learn to celebrate the smallest joys.

You will eventually find your voice, and public speaking will become your passion. I know that comes as a shock, since you have always been terrified to speak in front of people. Believe it or not, your words will matter. You will write many words, and people will read them and ask for more.

Young Janet, I am the older, wiser you. I bear the scars of your bad decisions. I get to celebrate your accomplishments, ones you never imagined possible. The refinement was painful. Here's the thing. All this has made me, the older Janet, more empathetic, sympathetic, and wise.

I am the seventy-year-old Janet. You made me who I am today. It's been quite the wild adventure.

***

What advice would you give your younger self?

What mistake or detour taught you the most?

What lessons have you learned, and how have those lessons changed you?

When I'm Overwhelmed

What do a hymn, scripture, and a prayer have in common? They soothe my weary heart and calm my soul.

When life gets too much and I am overwhelmed, I turn to those three things. They settle my anxiety and give me a soft place to lay down my burdens.

I've often said, "I can name that hymn in five notes." It wasn't only that I have been singing hymns since I was a child, but also that I was a church organist and pianist for much of my life.

Give me a sweet hymn that takes me back to the church of my childhood, and not only does my voice sing, but so does my heart.

"Victory in Jesus," "When the Roll Is Called Up Yonder," "In the Garden," "He Touched Me," and "The Old Rugged Cross."

I could name hundreds of hymns. They were the songs upon which I built my Faith. I sang about God's promises and learned from the hymns that Faith could move mountains and calm my soul's anxiety.

I was raised on hymns that pointed me to Jesus and led me to the altar, where He not only saved my soul but also gave my life and its sufferings a purpose.

My mother not only took me to church; she was often my Sunday School teacher. Mom didn't have a high school education, but she was ever so wise. She knew her Scripture. Back in the day, when she was growing up in Sunnybrook, Kentucky, kids were needed at home on the farm. The girls took care of the younger children and the elderly in the family. My grandparents had ten girls and one boy. Mom was in the middle. There weren't many hobbies back then, so... there were eleven children.

Mom had us memorize scripture in our Sunday School class. We had no idea we would need those verses when we grew up. We were building a foundation to stand on when the hurricanes of life left us battered and worn. We didn't just sing "Standing on the Promises of God"—we learned to live them.

> I can do everything through him who gives me strength. (Philippians 4:13)

> Remember the earlier days after you had received the light, when you endured in a great conflict full of suffering. (Hebrews 10:32)

So do not throw away your confidence; it will be richly rewarded. You need to persevere so that when you have done the will of God, you will receive what he has promised. For, in just a little while, he who is coming will come and will not delay. (Hebrews 10:35-37)

And of course, the 23rd Psalm: "Even though I walk through the darkest valley, I will fear no evil, for you are with me."

Years later, I came to realize it was not just a physical death but also the death of relationships, careers, and dreams. The Good Shepherd always walked with me, and His Scriptures spoke to me. Psalm 23 and the hymn "In the Garden" reminded me.

We prayed "God is great, God is good" over meals. We prayed "Now I lay me down to sleep" at bedtime. Simple prayers that would someday lead to complicated ones.

"Lord, help me trust You when I don't understand why You are allowing this to happen. Help me see the good that comes from this unfair trial."

The fact is, not all of my prayers were answered the way I wanted. I was the girl who obeyed the Ten Commandments of the Bible and the fifty-two of my church. Okay, that last number may have been an exaggeration, but if you grew up in a very conservative church, you understand.

So many nights, I pulled the covers up over my shoulders and prayed that things would get better. Sometimes they did. Sometimes they didn't. However, I began to see God working in my life in ways that left me shaking my head and telling God, "That was You who brought that scripture or song to my mind to encourage my heart and calm my soul."

When I prayed the Lord's Prayer and asked for daily bread, I came to see that "bread" wasn't just physical nourishment I needed for the day but also spiritual nourishment.

The hymns held me fast as hurt, discouragement, fear, worries, and battles wreaked havoc on my life. I sang worship songs with my hands lifted high. "Great is Thy Faithfulness" became a battle cry.

Scripture told me time and time again how much God loved me and had a plan for my life.

> For I know the plans I have for you, declares the Lord, plans
> to prosper you and not to harm you, plans to give you a hope
> and a future. (Jeremiah 29:11)

After seven decades, I can tell you one thing—okay, lots of things. But the main thing is this: the little girl who knelt at the altar when she was seven had no idea what her tomorrows would bring, but accepting Jesus as her Savior was the best decision she ever made.

Every hymn, every scripture, every prayer has been a cornerstone of my Faith. They gave me strength when life shook me to my core.

There is joy to be found in a hymn. Joy actually gives strength to the weary. There is wisdom in the Scriptures that gives me hope. There is power in prayer as I exercise my Faith to believe that God hears my prayers. While He may not answer them the way I want, He will walk alongside me every day.

***

What is your favorite hymn that is your go-to when you need your joy bucket filled?

What scripture is your go-to for wisdom?

When is it difficult for you to pray, "Thy will be done?"

The Power of a Gentle Voice

You have the right to remain silent. Anything you say can and probably will be used against you. You are not under arrest, but you may face the consequences of your words.

Can you relate?

You want to speak up and say something, but something inside says, "Don't do it." Oh, but you want to share your thoughts. They need to hear your thoughts. Sometimes you have to be brave and do things while fear sits ever so close, poking its daggers into your tender heart.

That same feeling often comes when I am writing. Will what I have to say change their opinions? Honestly, I doubt it. In this day and age, it seems so many people have their feet and their minds stuck in cement. They aren't going to budge. They don't ever think they could be wrong.

What if I write something that opens even a small crack, so people might think differently? Do I dare? Will it stop people from reading what I have to say? Will they stop liking me? Do I dare say, "Let them?"

I often sit with a bit of fear and trepidation as I write my opinion column for the *Hamilton County Reporter*. I enjoy writing fun, happy columns, but I can't do that every week. And yes, people need to smile and even laugh. I hope to help people think beyond their own thoughts.

When I sit down to write, I don't always know where my thoughts will take me. I pray each week that God will direct my thoughts and fingertips.

We live in a day and age when we can be overwhelmed by the news. People are so loud with their opinions. Give them a microphone, and their voices get louder. I don't want to be loud or argumentative. I write with a gentle voice, hoping my words are heard and embraced with the grace with which they are said. I pray my words matter. As I've mentioned, I want the epitaph on my gravestone to read, "Her words mattered."

> A gentle response defuses anger, but a sharp tongue kindles a temper-fire. Knowledge flows like spring water from the wise; fools are leaky faucets, dripping nonsense. (Proverbs 15:1–2 MSG)

> Truly I tell you, whatever you did not do for one of the least of these, you did not do for me. (Matthew 25:45)

My parents always taught me to look out for those who have no voice. Always stand up for those who look different, live their lives differently, and do not have my privileges.

If I don't use my voice for the less than, I am shrinking away from who I am supposed to be. That thought shakes me to my core. I will always err on the side of kindness.

I have the right to remain silent, but I will use my voice to stand with those who are often silenced. If you can't be kind, be silent. You have the right to voice your opinion, but if you use it to harm others... shame on you.

> Well-spoken words bring satisfaction; well-done work has its own reward. (Proverbs 12:14 MSG)

Enough said... for now.

***

When have you struggled with speaking up versus staying silent?

When have your words been used against you?

When have you wished you had spoken up and regretted not doing so?

From Let Them to Let Me Let Them

I never knew two words could be so powerful until I said and believed them.

How could a book not found on the Inspirational Christian genre shelves make such an impact on my life?

> Trust in the Lord with all your heart and lean not on your own understanding. (Proverbs 3:5)

God used the book, *The Let Them Theory* by Mel Robbins, to open my eyes to what He had been trying to show me.

Since I was a child, I have struggled with being a people pleaser. It started with pleasing my teachers, then my friends, especially the popular kids. It worsened as I grew older. I changed who I was to fit in.

What will people think? That question seemed to preface every decision. For some reason, I valued the opinion of others, even those whom I barely knew.

I not only cared about what others thought of me, but also got caught up in allowing them to treat me badly and accepted their bad behavior toward me as my fault.

After reading *The Let Them Theory*, I began to see things in a different light.

How precious to me are your thoughts, God! (Psalm 139:17)

It was what God thought of me and my serving Him in all ways that mattered. This was a huge revelation.

I wrote in my journal:

Let them not like me.

Let them believe what they want about me and say what they want about me.

Let them leave me out of being invited.

Let them not return my phone call or text message.

Let them rant, rave, and complain about something they think I should have done or not done. Let them try to gaslight me.

Let them disagree with me.

For so many years, I carried the weight of anxiety over what people might have been thinking about me. I was exhausted trying to figure out why I felt such a need to be liked, accepted, and cared about.

A gut-wrenching incident made me realize I had a toxic need to please others. Something was said to me that hurt me to the tenderest part of my heart, causing me many sleepless nights and more than a few tears. I knew I needed to figure out the intricacies of my need to please and be liked by everyone.

The person who said the hurtful words barely knew me. He wanted to believe what he thought was true. It wasn't. He refused to listen to my explanation. I was deemed guilty in the court of his opinion.

Some of you will not understand because you've never lived with this anxiety. Others are saying, "I so get this."

It was in the late fall of 2024 when I saw an advertisement to pre-order a book written by Mel Robbins. *The Let Them Theory* was scheduled for release in January 2025.

When it arrived on my doorstep, I could not have fathomed I would be opening such a treasure chest of words my heart needed to embrace. For three days, I sat in my reading chair, holding tightly to a highlighter. By the end of the third day, I closed the book and discarded the worn-out highlighter.

Though the highlighter was dry, my eyes were wet with tears. My heart felt like it had been wrung out like a washcloth. The anxiety, from which I had suffered, had a remedy. I no longer felt like I was being held hostage by the opinions and actions of others. I knew it would take effort on my part to embrace this new way of thinking. God had nudged me to order the book. I obeyed the nudge.

As I read, I felt as if I were sitting in a therapist's office. My eyes read the words, but my heart felt them.

For so long, I had allowed others' opinions to control me. I made so many decisions after asking, "What will people think?"

I gave away my power like Oprah Winfrey gave away cars at Christmas, "You get some power, and you get some power. Now, will you like me?"

I also gave away my peace of mind. I allowed my decisions to flow through a sieve of other people's opinions. It was both confusing and exhausting.

I now realize I cannot control what anyone thinks about me. The thing is, they have not walked in my shoes, nor do they have any idea what my journey has been like. They view my life through foggy goggles and distorted appearances. Their vision of me is not 20/20.

Off go the chains of the opinions of others. I'm no longer a slave to what others think I should be doing. I've been throwing away every hoop I've been handed to jump through. I no longer wait for others' opinions to validate my decisions.

I seek the wisdom of Scripture and pray,

> May these words of my mouth and this meditation of my heart be pleasing in your sight, Lord, my Rock and my Redeemer. (Psalm 19:14)

But there is more to the theory.

There is the "Let Me" aspect.

I cannot control people or their thoughts about me. I have to take responsibility for my life, relationships, and connections that are right for me. This is where peace is found.

When I say, "Let me," I am taking responsibility for what I do next. Let me have difficult conversations. Let me not waste my time debating insignificant issues.

Let me be kind and considerate of others' feelings, but not at the expense of my peace.

The "Let Me" theory does not change how I treat others; **it changes how I treat myself**.

> Search me, God, and know my heart; test me and know my anxious thoughts. (Psalm 139:23)

God knows my thoughts and the reasons for my actions and decisions. I pray, and I stay sensitive to His nudges.

Obeying the nudge to order Mel Robbins' book has been life-changing.

If you read the cover of Mel Robbins' book, you will see it says, *A Life-Changing Tool That Millions of People Can't Stop Talking About*. I don't know about millions, but I do know about one. That one is me.

If people disagree with my thoughts or decisions, that is on them. I'm no longer a slave to the opinion of others. I find myself calmer and more content. I'm not constantly explaining my decisions or thoughts unless I feel it is necessary.

I've even been known to walk away from someone who is waiting for an argument. My silence brings the discussion to a close. I might add that this really feels good at times.

I also have the thought that God is saying, "Atta girl, Janet, you are finally understanding what I want you to know."

The book, *The Let Them Theory*, won't be found on the shelves of Christian Inspiration, but I'm so thankful I obeyed God's nudge and ordered it. God certainly does work in strange and mysterious ways… if we obey Him, or in other words… Let Him.

> And the peace of God, which transcends all understanding, will guard your hearts and your minds in Christ Jesus. (Philippians 4:7)

***

Make your own "Let Them" list just like I did. What do you need to let go of?

Now create a "Let Me" list. What responsibility are you taking back for your own peace and decisions?

What "nudge" have you been ignoring that might lead to your own freedom?

The Power of Five

When my grandson, Jake Baker, graduated from high school, I wanted to give him something no one else could, so I shared my thoughts on how he could build habits that would help him succeed in life. I shared them in my newspaper column and had no idea how far-reaching they would be. It seemed mothers and grandmothers were copying them to give to their graduates. And so, I share these with you.

The Power of Five.

Do five intentional things every morning to create purpose for your day.

1. Make your bed. This creates order.

2. Pray for wisdom. This creates a mindset for any decisions you have to make.

3. Make a list of five things you want to accomplish. Keep the list simple. This creates intentionality.

4. Send a text to encourage a friend. Your words matter. Never doubt the power of a word of encouragement.

5. Leave your room/apartment/home in order. Coming home to a calm environment, rather than to clutter and chaos, helps keep the mind relaxed. Take five minutes to put away "stuff."

Show kindness in five ways each day.

1. Smile at five strangers. Yours may be the only smile they get that day. A smile tells someone they are seen.

2. Speak to the older adult standing in line with you. You may be the only one to speak to them. They need to feel seen.

3. Pat a buddy on the back, fist-bump him, and offer a word of praise or encouragement. He may be hiding a hurt or worry.

4. Ask your server how their day is going. Listen to what they say. People want to be seen and heard while doing their job. It may be almost as important as the tip you leave them.

5. Tell someone you appreciate them and why. Words of appreciation hug the heart.

Consider who is in your Circle of Five.

Did you know that the five people you spend the most time with significantly influence the person you become? Pick and choose your friends well.

1. People of integrity

2. Kind people

3. People who are not critical or mean

4. People who have goals

5. People who make good decisions and take responsibility for their mistakes

Guard your reputation.

1. Leave fifteen minutes earlier than planned. This gives space for traffic issues or delays. You become known for being where you are supposed to be, and being on time shows that you value others' time.

2. Learn the importance of a sincere apology. Apologies need to be followed up with a change. Actions really do speak louder than words. Written apologies are pure gold.

3. Take responsibility for your mistakes. You will make them. People notice your willingness to take responsibility more than your perfection.

4. Your word is only as good as your reputation, so be truthful. Once you are caught in a lie, your reputation is tainted. You can't cover manure with any amount of perfume and expect it not to stink.

5. You are known by the company you keep. (Back to your Circle of Five)

Take time to breathe at the end of your day.

1. Take five deep breaths and slowly release them to calm your nervous system.

2. Name five things that made your day sweet: Coffee with a friend. Your favorite song on the radio. You heard a child's laughter. You caught more

green lights than red. Your grandmother sent you a text saying she loves you.

3. Name five things you are grateful for: Chick-fil-A. A full tank of gas. A buddy who gets your jokes. Clean laundry. Tickets to a concert with friends.

4. Reflect on a favorite scripture and why it's a favorite. Write it down.

5. Say your prayers. Thank God for getting you through a bad day or celebrating a good one.

This may sound like a lot to remember, but it will become a way of life. It will become routine.

You won't intentionally think about having to do any of it—well, except the cleaning-up-your-stuff part. It all leads to a pretty simple but quite sweet life.

The Power of Five is life-changing if you choose to accept its challenges.

> Commit your way to the Lord; trust in Him and he will do this. (Psalm 37:5)

***

What is your morning routine?

Is it serving you well? What could you change to make it serve you better based on the Power of Five?

Who are the five people you consider your Tribe of Five?

Do you make your bed every day? (I had to ask.)

The Power of Ponderings

At the beginning of each year, I do not make a resolution; instead, I make a list of ten things I learned the previous year. I call them the Golden Ponderings.

Here's what I learned the year I turned seventy.

#10 We're all just doing our best to figure out how to live our best lives.

The older I get, the "best" looks different. It goes at a slower pace. I've become more of a noticer. You have to slow down to really notice what is special about every day. I plan to write down one thing I "notice" that is good each day. Some days there will be more than one. Most will be simple things.

#9 Each of us shows love differently.

We need to learn to give our family and friends the grace to do so. Why do we complicate relationships by insisting on how we want to be loved? Let them love us in the ways they know how. Period.

#8 Slather grace over everyone you love.

Don't let your expectations paint an unrealistic picture of your relationships. This might blend into number nine a bit.

#7 Spending time with those you love is the greatest gift of all.

Time is a hugger of the heart. An invitation is truly a gift. It tells others you value their presence in your life. If you invite them into your home, let go of the idea that your house needs to look perfect. People just want to feel included, heard, and seen. They do not care about your dust.

#6 Taking a walk relaxes your mind and helps you step away from the demands of the day, putting things into perspective.

Walking is both mental and physical therapy. Don't we all need a little therapy? Some of us need a lot. Do not be ashamed to seek a therapist—your mental health matters.

#5 Your soul needs music.

When you listen, it opens your heart to joy. When you sing, it swings open the door to even more joy. You may sing off-key, but your heart doesn't care.

#4 Let people think what they think and do what they do.

You must decide to... Let them. You cannot change them. Please don't let their problems ruin your day.

#3 Walking away from a conversation says it all.

Not engaging in an argument is sometimes not only the best thing to do but also the loudest statement. Walking away is like putting an exclamation point on your thoughts. They know.

#2 Quiet love speaks volumes.

Your husband makes you a cup of coffee and knows exactly how you like it. Sending a text that says, "Have I told you lately?" Sitting across from your husband and quietly praying for him while he watches the third football game of the day. I call these things quiet slatherings of love.

#1 Kindness matters.

In a world where loud chaos and pure meanness are the news of the day, kindness matters. Look for the kind words people share. Look for the everyday gestures of kindness. Look for ways to be kind. Your heart, as well as the people you encounter, will thank you. Don't let the loud voices make you mean. Be nice to the ugly, and don't let their ugliness make you ugly. Pretty is as pretty does is something my mother taught me. Ugly is as ugly does, and it's also true. In a world full of ugly, be pretty. Nothing will ever be as pretty as kindness.

I tuck this list where I can find it throughout the year. It keeps me centered and my soul filled with good things to remember when life gets heavy and overwhelming.

***

How could keeping a list like this help you?

What's the most important lesson you learned last year?

How will this lesson help you better navigate this year?

Lead Me Not to be a Fixer

My name is Janet, and I am a "fixer."

Tell me your troubles, and before you finish, I'll already be in "fix-it" mode. I'm thinking about how I can help, what I can say to encourage you, what needs to be done, and how we move forward.

Some things can't be fixed, at least not by me. That is hard to grasp for someone who is both empathetic and sympathetic to a fault.

Empathy: the action of understanding, being aware of, and being sensitive to the feelings, thoughts, and experiences of others.

Sympathy: a feeling or expression of sincere concern for someone who is going through something difficult or painful.

Here I am wearing my invisible cape, ready to save the day.

I sometimes put myself in a position I'm not supposed to be in. Let me explain.

1. Someone just needs me to listen while they vent or to voice what their heart needs to say.

They're not asking me to fix the problem; they're just asking me to sit and listen. This is a challenge for a "fixer" like me.

2. Sometimes I'm just supposed to provide the soup.

I need to show up with a bit of nourishment and an encouraging word. I need to take off my invisible hero cape, put on an invisible apron, fix the soup, and sit a spell to let them talk.

3. I am a "fixer," which can also make me an enabler.

Enabler: one who enables another to persist in self-destructive behavior by providing excuses or by making it possible to avoid the consequences of that behavior.

4. The most difficult thing for a "fixer" is wanting to fix someone you love and finding it impossible to do so.

Did you know there is such a thing as fixer syndrome? It is a compulsive, often anxiety-driven need to solve others' problems, frequently at the expense of one's own well-being and boundaries. Setting boundaries can be a challenge for those with fixer syndrome. This author/fixer knows this well. I see her in the mirror every morning.

I want to make things easier for others. On occasion, I have taken on burdens I was never meant to bear. This has led me to believe I can be someone's savior. I cannot be their savior. That took me a long time to realize.

Taking on burdens that I was never meant to bear led me to the brink of mental and emotional exhaustion. I believe that my body recognizes it as trauma.

I've learned that sometimes I just have to put others' burdens in a basket and hand them over to the one and only Savior, who is Jesus.

Jesus, I know You love this person more than I do. I hand them over to You. Guard their heart. Bring others into their life who can help lead them to You. Help them overcome whatever they are facing and show them who You can be in their life. Help me set boundaries where needed and reassure me that I have done all I can. Amen.

It's not an easy prayer for a fixer to pray. A fixer has a tender heart. Saying "no" to someone you care about feels mean and anything but caring. Allowing someone you love to fail is one of the hardest things a "fixer" will ever do. You can reassure a fixer with encouraging words like: "You have done your best. This is hard, but it's for their good in the long run. You can't control what anyone does or how they feel about you." Sadly, the inner voice of a fixer is louder. It tells her she is a failure in so many ways.

A fixer never feels like they are doing enough. I wish I had more answers that weren't so challenging and just plain hard, but I don't. I'm still trying to work through *not* being a fixer. It may be something I deal with until my last breath.

I think the strongest person in the room is the one who wants to fix everything but doesn't. She just holds onto her Faith, and even when she can't fix everything and everyone, her soul can say, "It is well."

***

What situations or relationships trigger your need to "fix" things?

Describe a time when you carried a burden you weren't meant to carry.

When has someone taken advantage of your good heart?

How did you respond, and what would you do differently now?

Declining the Invitation

I was invited to the argument. It was one I didn't see coming. He took a virtual seat at my table. He actually texted me. He wanted me to join a debate.

May these words of my mouth and this meditation of my heart be pleasing in your sight, Lord, my Rock and my Redeemer. (Psalm 19:14)

The wisdom of this scripture reminds me to keep my thoughts to myself and to refrain from saying what my lips and my fingertips want to say. It is easier said than done.

The words I read pushed my buttons. I quickly found the words I wanted to say. Nope, not going to respond. I was so tempted. My words were justified, or so I thought.

I've learned that the enemy comes to steal my peace and my joy—if I allow it.

Priscilla Shirer, one of my favorite Bible study teachers, says, "You've been letting offense sit at your table like it pays rent." Can I get an AMEN?

When I am offended and respond defensively, I open the door to anger, frustration, and an ongoing battle. On occasion, I might have said, "You can't argue with the back end of a donkey."

Scripture tells me that knowing who God is in my life makes it possible to have peace that passes all understanding. I don't have to react in anger, defending my thoughts or my position. I can choose my battles.

Sometimes the best reaction is to walk away from a confrontation. When people have no one to argue with, **they lose their power**. Read that again and maybe highlight it.

Let them be wrong. Let them think whatever they want.

What if they turn others against me? Those who care about me know my heart, and most would defend me. If they don't, then that's on them.

The enemy wants to keep my emotions stirred up. The enemy wants me to dwell on the negative, the criticism, and the wrongs done to me.

I believe the enemy wants me to question the whys behind the comments that offend. Why did she say that? Why was she included and not I? Why didn't she save me a seat?

When I allow offense to sit at my table, I am served bitterness and resentment. The longer I let the offense linger, the harder it is to regain my peace. Negative comments sink me into the quicksand of defeat and hurt.

It is when I stop pedaling with my emotions and coast, knowing who God is in my life, that I can become calm and peaceful.

The enemy aims to distract, divide, and destroy. The enemy recognizes my weaknesses. More than once, while on a walk, I stop and say, "Get thee behind me, satan!" Those words reclaim my power.

When I am emotionally worn down, I get distracted and don't notice who or what is sitting at my table. The longer the offense sits there, the more power it has over me. Petty offenses escalate into greater aggravations, and anger follows me to bed, keeping me awake as I toss and turn. I wrestle with the covers and with what I should have said. I plan my next conversation.

But oh, there is such beauty when I can hold my tongue, plan no further conversation, and pray that God will deliver me from any evil I might be a part of. This includes the desire to jerk a knot in their tail. No matter what I want to believe, a harsh word serves no purpose.

God's Word gives me power over any offense, hurtful words, or unfairness. I can choose not to be held hostage by bitterness. I can break free from the chains of others' opinions. I can rise above the ugly situational quicksand that wants to drown me.

I must keep my mind on who gives me a peace that passes all understanding. I remember the song "The Battle Belongs to the Lord." God designed me to handle whatever the enemy throws at me. The enemy doesn't attack what isn't a threat. My peace and joy are where I find my strength. The enemy knows that, so he finds ways (and people) to ruffle my feathers.

> And the peace of God, which transcends all understanding,
> will guard your hearts and your minds in Christ Jesus.
> (Philippians 4:7)

Offense has been asked to leave my table. Anger and retaliation are no longer options. Being easily offended no longer has power over me. Peace and joy have been invited back. They will always be invited to my table.

***

What do you think about being invited to an argument and not engaging in it?

What keeps you from speaking your mind when attacked?

Describe a time when you regretted saying something in the heat of the moment.

The Power of Words

"The words we speak become the house we live in." —Hafiz

Those words, written by the Persian poet Hafiz in the 1300s, have circulated the world for hundreds of years and remain true today.

Our words construct the life in which we live.

Our thoughts echo in everything we do and determine how we spend our day. Our thoughts become our spoken words, and those words lead to our actions.

We either bring a positive or a negative attitude to our days. We all have days when we are consumed by the gut punches of the nightly news or by family issues that put the *dys* in the best of functional families.

Some people walk into a room, and you can feel their gloom and doom. Others walk into a room, and you feel the glitter and confetti in their words. Some of the happiest people have stories that break my heart. They embrace the moment. What a way to live.

Negative thoughts, if left long enough, can become cemented in our brains. We all know people who wouldn't recognize a positive word if they tripped over it. Okay, that might be an exaggeration, but you get what I am saying. They bring to the table, or the coffee shop, or the discussion, every reason why something, if it is not their idea, won't work or will go wrong. Don't you just love serving on a committee with them? (Read that last sentence with sarcasm.)

Then there are the positive people in our lives who bring solutions, confidence, and excitement to those situations. They are open to new ideas. They share their excitement about all they are a part of. Don't you just want to dance with them? You want to invite them to everything you are a part of.

Negative people put a damper on everything. You see them walk into a room, and you think, well, this won't be fun. Have you ever known someone who always seems to leave a not-so-pleasant aroma in a conversation? They bring sour grapes and an attitude that gives off vibes as stinky as Limburger cheese into any conversation where they are not getting their way.

With age comes wisdom. Mark Twain said it well: "Never argue with stupid people; they will drag you down to their level and then beat you with experience."

Some people are born arguers. I've learned some words to say to make a quick exit from their table: "I don't think my thoughts are needed at this table." You don't have to argue to get your point across.

My dear brothers and sisters, take note of this: Everyone should be quick to listen, slow to speak and slow to become angry. (James 1:19)

I enjoy sitting at a table with a diversity of people from different backgrounds, with different thoughts, interests, and ages. I do my best to come with an open mind and be willing to listen—I mean, really listen—not just waiting for the chance to share my thoughts. I give what they say a chance to be pondered before I share my thoughts. It's not always easy. Age, along with a bit of experience, has made it easier.

Sometimes I do realize it is not necessary to speak at all. Oh, that's a difficult one for me.

> Those who consider themselves religious and yet do not keep a tight rein on their tongues deceive themselves, and their religion is worthless. (James 1:26)

My passion for writing is all about words. With my words, I want to express my thoughts that build others up, and by doing so, I know "my house" is a happy place. I pray "my house" will always be a place of refuge, peace, and harmony, sprinkled with words of love and acceptance.

May the words I speak be a wonderful place to live.

***

How do you handle being around someone who is always negative?

When is it hard for you to really listen instead of planning what to say next?

What kind of "house" are your words building?

Finding Joy in the Quiet

To be **quiet.** To not be distracted by the noise of the day. It's not just about silence.

We don't have to focus on the noise, even if it is there.

Joy can be found in the quiet if we are deliberate about our focus. I'm talking about settling your thoughts, worries, and the voice of chaos. Do you have those in your life? I sure do.

My high school teacher, Mr. David Purvis, shared this quote with me: "To dwell on the past is to court depression. To dwell on the future is to court anxiety." Oh, my goodness, is that not profound? *This* is the reason we are to live in the moment. *This* is why I have learned to seek joy in the quiet morning of my day.

Did you know that moments of joy awaken endorphins (happy hormones) in your body, acting as natural feel-good chemicals that can improve your mood and put you in a positive state of mind?

I often write about getting up early, before the sun peeks in my kitchen window. I sit at my kitchen table, sipping my Highlander Grog coffee with a bit of Chobani Sweet Cream and basking in the quiet. When I start my day with this ritual, I find myself happier throughout the day.

My mother sat on her front porch and rocked in her rocking chair. She once told me that as you get older, you appreciate the sounds you hear when you are quiet. She loved listening to the birds, the laughter of the neighborhood kids, and the dueling lawnmowers of her neighbors, who seemed to synchronize their mowing.

Mom said that when you are quiet, you can smell the scent of flowers in a way you usually ignore. That is something to ponder.

It has taken me years to perfect my ability to embrace the quiet.

Those happy hormones also give me a sense of peace. I'm not struggling to figure out what I should be doing. The moments of quiet contemplation as I read from my Bible and one of my devotional books set the tone of my day.

> You are my refuge and my shield; I have put my hope in your word. (Psalm 119:114)

Have you ever considered why the twenty-third Psalm says, "He leads me beside quiet waters?" God wants us to rest and be quiet. You may be like me and wake up ready to tackle your day like a Kung Fu fighter.

I can choose to wake up and hear in my mind, "Lady, start your engine," and I'm off to the races of the day. I'm overwhelmed and tired before I even put on my running shoes. I do not run, but if you ever see me running, please know that a bee or a clown is chasing me. I fear both.

Learning to be quiet at the beginning of my day has been life-changing.

When reading my devotion, I often play an old hymn or a worship song. CeCe Winans can take me to church when she sings "Come, Jesus, Come." Oh, the sweet joy of the rivers of Grace of which she sings.

Starting my day like this gives me strength and focus.

In the quiet, I welcome God into my day. Something about His presence casts out fear and discouragement—even if my prayers aren't answered, even in the waiting, even though the day is hard. He walks with me as a shepherd tends to his sheep; God tends to me.

You can choose to believe or not, but I've been on the frontlines of life's fiercest battles, and I know that starting my day with a time of quiet helps prepare me for whatever the day throws at me.

Joy is a shield. My Faith holds the shield before me. Where there is joy, there is hope. Joy untangles the messiness of my hardest days. Don't think for a minute I don't have them.

I will continue to find joy in the quiet of my early mornings and on my back porch while rocking. I can hear my mother saying, "I told you so."

***

What does your quiet time look like?

What brings you joy in the morning?

What does basking in the quiet look like to you?

Don't Be Ugly

"Janet Kay, don't you be ugly." I can still hear my mother saying those words to me when I was a little girl. They had nothing to do with my looks and everything to do with my actions and words. I was taught not to use ugly cuss words. I was taught that everyone deserves our kindness. I was taught to be like Jesus.

As a newspaper columnist and author, I feel a great responsibility to never be ugly in any way with my words. I want my words to bring hope and joy to those who are hurting. I want my words to shine a light in a dark world. As a Jesus follower, I want to show people who Jesus can be in their lives.

Above all else, Jesus was kind and loving. He didn't hang out with the rich and powerful. He sought out the outcasts, those whose lifestyles led to their being shunned. I want to be like Jesus.

I remember seeing the words in my mother's Bible that were written in red. That meant those words were spoken by Jesus:

So in everything, do to others what you would have them do to you. (Matthew 7:12)

> Truly I tell you, whatever you did not do for one of the least of these, you did not do for me. (Matthew 25:45)

His words were all-inclusive.

> Love one another. As I have loved you, so you must love one another. By this everyone will know that you are my disciples, if you love one another. (John 13:34-35)

I love the way The Message Bible reads in 1 Corinthians 13:1: "If I speak with human eloquence and angelic ecstasy but don't love, I'm nothing but the creaking of a rusty gate."

I pray I am never like a rusty gate.

Mom, you taught me well.

***

What is a funny expression that your mother said to you?

How do you feel challenged to love those who are not like you, and how do you go about loving them?

How do your friends influence who and how you love others?

Meandering Thoughts

Starting Something New

"I have no idea what I am doing, but it's not going to stop me."

How many times have I said those words? Too many to count.

I know some people are full of giggly anticipation whenever they begin something new. They are ready to dive in headfirst and come up soaking in every bit of what a new thing brings, whether it's a new year, a new job, a new relationship, or a new adventure.

And then there's me.

I'm more like a big toe, slowly dipping into the newness. I do that at the beach. I do not like to get my hair wet. That may go back to when I had permed big hair in the 1980s. Anything new takes me a while to adjust to and feel comfortable.

Trying something new makes me feel awkward and clumsy. I'm always thinking, "Who will see me, and will I look like a dork?" Do you feel that way too?

If I'm being totally honest, I also fear failure because I don't want to disappoint people. I don't want to imagine them saying, "Bless her heart.

She tried, but it's not as good as we thought it would be." I hope my fears about this second book aren't warranted. I want you to like me, really like me—at least my words, anyway. If you love Sally Field, you know what I mean, from her iconic "You Like Me!" speech at the 57th Oscars for *Places in the Heart.*

Even when I walk into a room full of new people, I hear the voices in my head say, "You won't fit in. You don't belong in this room. You're not good enough." Maybe you, too, have heard those voices. They are loud and mean.

When I was forced to find a new doctor after having the same one for over thirty years, I asked all my friends for recommendations. It wasn't so much about feeling confident that they would do their due diligence in overseeing my healthcare needs, but if you are a woman reading this, you know that undressing and having your "glory" parts checked is uncomfortable, to say the least. If you're under the age of sixty, you need to know that when you are over sixty, the medical field does not care about your "glory" parts. Insurance will not cover those parts during your checkups. I searched and found a doctor who seemed to be everything I was looking for. At our first meeting, I asked her not to retire until I passed. She's quite young. So far, so good.

As I have gotten older, I do not get excited about getting anything new that involves technology. I recently had to buy a new washer. I walked into the big blue store and told Rex, my go-to appliance guy, that I wanted the best, simplest washer they had. I did not want it to tell me the time of day or sing to me. I wanted it to wash with an agitator and make a simple noise when it was finished. He pointed to the one he said he would buy. Funny thing is, when I first used it, I discovered it plays a simple little tune when it's finished. It also has a window to watch the clothes wash. I have wondered if anyone actually watches. It's much better than my old one, which had a screaming buzzer when the cycle finished. I purchased the matching dryer. It plays the same little tune. It's the little things in life that make my heart smile, like a washer and dryer that play a duet.

When my husband and I got married, he asked me why I never used my dishwasher. I told him it didn't work. He asked how long it had been since it worked. I told him fourteen years. I then explained that when you are single, you don't spend money unless it's necessary. I washed dishes by hand until a new one arrived. I love my husband. A new dishwasher told me I was cherished. It was an unfamiliar feeling, that of being cherished by a man.

At fifty-eight, I began a new life with Chuck Leonard. To say that God certainly fulfilled a promise He made to me during my devotions one day is an understatement.

> Forget the former things; do not dwell on the past. See, I am doing a new thing! Now it springs up; do you not perceive it? I am making a way in the wilderness and streams in the wasteland. (Isaiah 43:18-19)

For fourteen years, I was single. I claimed that promise on October 8, 2012, and it is recorded in my Bible. I met my husband, Chuck Leonard, in the waiting room where I worked in August 2013. We were married on February 23, 2014. I had to let go of my past hurts and disappointments to find all that God had prepared for me with Chuck Leonard. Oh, my goodness, did God do a new thing!

***

When have you been full of fear and trepidation as you started something new?

How did your Faith sustain you?

Do you look back now and see that God certainly did have a plan for your life?

Meandering Thoughts

Growing up as a little girl in the 1960s taught me the joy of simple pleasures. I smile as I write about them. I loved Sundays, and I still do.

A typical Sunday would find my mother and me in the pews at the little Nazarene Church on the corner of Tenth and Grant Streets. Sunday School at 9:30 and Worship at 11:00. To this day, whenever I hear an old Gospel hymn, my heart smiles: "Amazing Grace," "Victory in Jesus," "When the Roll Is Called Up Yonder," "Great Is Thy Faithfulness," "Just as I Am." There is something about a hymn that affirms my relationship with God.

When we returned home, Mom tied on her apron and started making biscuits and gravy. She fried the sausage until it was a bit crispy, the way my dad liked it. Dad didn't attend church regularly until, as he would say, "he found the Lord" as his Savior at fifty-two.

We climbed into the family Oldsmobile after the dishes were done. Mom never left dirty dishes in the sink, and my parents always drove an Oldsmobile. We took rides and meandered through the winding country roads of Hamilton County, Indiana. We always ended up driving over the old, covered Potters Bridge. I can still hear the sound of the wooden planks. Thuda. Thuda. Thuda. Yes, *thuda* is a sound.

On hot summer Sundays, we visited the Blue Ribbon Dairy, which served the best ice cream. Strawberry ripple or lime sherbet were my favorites, always two scoops. Dad and Mom ordered butter pecan.

It's funny the things you remember from your childhood.

I remember stopping to pick up a few Hedge apples (Osage oranges). Mom always said they were poisonous. If you want to know more, Google it. They are fascinating.

As we drove by certain houses, we expected to see families on their porches, visiting with neighbors or friends who often dropped by without advance notice. We were sometimes those friends.

If my parents ever gave directions, they rarely included the names of roads or streets. It was more like, "Turn left at Grandpa's Candy Store, drive a few blocks until you see the library. Turn right. Cross the White River and go up the hill. The hospital will be on your left." Those kinds of directions rarely got anyone lost. Of course, back then, we had fewer places to get lost.

If we had time before evening services at church, we all took a nap. Sundays felt truly sacred, not just in church but in the day's meanderings. A Sunday afternoon Nazarene nap was good for the body as well as the soul. It still is today.

During the Sunday night services, I heard many hymns and testimonies. People stood to share what the Lord had done for them that week, affirming that the Lord worked in strange and mysterious ways. I heard stories of Faith and remembered them long after the saints reached Heaven. A few people in the congregation were a bit "funny-turned," as my mother would say. I never could figure out why Brother Taylor felt skinny ties were a sin or why Brother Butcher walked the middle aisle of the church as he testified. Let's just say he could never whisper or use his inside voice when he testified. I've seen many a saintly woman wave her hanky while we sang, "What a day that will be when my Jesus I shall see." We sang that song at my mother's Celebration of Life.

We had both spring and fall revivals where our souls were blessed, and we found ourselves at the altar, making sure all our sins were covered by the blood. When I was little, I didn't understand much about sin, but I wanted to make sure mine were covered.

These meandering thoughts are sacred, at least to me. My salvation was found at the altar of the little Nazarene Church in Noblesville, Indiana. My Faith has many stories to tell. If you wonder why I capitalize Faith, it's because it's so important to me.

As my thoughts meander back to those Sacred Sundays, my heart smiles, and my soul is blessed as I remember.

I love when my thoughts take me back to the place where I first saw the Light, and the burdens of my heart are still being rolled away.

> "For I know the plans I have for you," declares the Lord, "plans to prosper you and not to harm you, plans to give you hope and a future. Then you will call on me and come pray to me, and I will listen to you. You will seek me and find me when you seek me with all your heart." (Jeremiah 29:11–13)

I had no idea about the plans God had for me when I asked Him into my heart at the altar at age seven, but He is still giving me hope and a future to this very day.

***

What role did the church or Faith play in your childhood Sundays?

What do you remember about sweet Sunday afternoons?

What hymns hug your heart?

Finding Heavenly Peace

"Let the calm of your soul seep into the chaos of your circumstances instead of letting the chaos of your circumstances seep into the calm of your soul." —Kelly Callen Heath

Have you ever felt as if your world were being shaken like a snow globe? Has there ever been a time when life no longer looked the same and nothing made sense? I know all too well how this feels. There were events in my life that shook me to my core.

Yet, my soul rests in the calm of knowing who God is in my life. It's something I've learned over time, despite the many snow globe shakes in my life.

TRUST: Reliance on the character, ability, strength, or truth of someone.

PEACE: Freedom from being disturbed or bothered by people or circumstances I cannot control. It is a state of security.

Trust in the Lord with all of your heart and lean not on your own understanding. (Proverbs 3:5)

Peace I leave with you; my peace I give you. I do not give to you as the world gives. Do not let your heart be troubled and do not be afraid. (John 14:27)

There have been times in my life when I had to make a difficult decision. I had to choose whether to believe that God was good or to lose my Faith. I signed divorce papers. I felt as if I had failed as a mother. I watched someone I loved lose their battle with cancer. I had to give up the decorating business I loved.

What do I do when I need to process my peace? I usually go for a walk. My favorite time to walk is early in the morning, before the day's noise and chaos begin. For some reason, I can gather, process, and sort my anxious thoughts and feelings of weariness much better while I'm walking.

As I walk, I begin to talk to God and to quote Scripture. All those verses I memorized as a child and the scriptures I read in Bible study have become an anchor when life feels scary or when I am hurting.

Other days, I listen to worship music or a Bible study lesson as I find my way around my neighborhood. Earbuds are a blessing. I try to notice at least five things that make me smile.

Heavenly Peace is hard to explain, yet I know it's there. If I hadn't faced adversity and trials, I wouldn't know such peace. It's a peace that can only be found in knowing who God is in my life.

Adversity throws us "under the circumstances." It's a scary place. My mind searches for escape as it imagines the worst that could happen. My body tenses, my chest tightens, and my breathing becomes labored.

Perhaps I imagine the worst because I have a history of it. I go straight to the worst-case scenario. I've written about some of them, but there are others I'll just call thorns in my flesh. Paul wrote in the New Testament about having a thorn in his flesh. He never specified what it was. Neither will I.

An angel appeared to Mary, then to Joseph, and then to the shepherds, saying, "Fear not." We can still hear those words when our worries and circumstances shake our world.

It's still difficult to describe experiencing Heavenly Peace when you are up to your neck in chaos. You go about your day, fighting the fog of bewilderment and the pain of so many unanswered questions. Yet...

> And the peace of God, which passes all understanding, will guard your hearts and your minds in Christ Jesus. (Philippians 4:7)

I felt that peace when I signed the papers declaring I was no longer loved. July 5, 2000.

I felt peace while standing in the hall of my mother's healthcare facility when the funeral home came to collect her body. December 17, 2020.

I felt peace when my heart broke in May 2022. It's not my story to tell, but the thorn still causes much pain.

I love walking in the peaceful hours of the morning. Add some snow flurries, and it's even better. I reflect on a baby born in a manger, in circumstances that make no sense. What a strange way to save the world.

At the end of the day, I can lay my head on my pillow and truly sleep in Heavenly Peace.

Thank you to my friend Kelly, who reminded me to let the calm of my soul seep into my circumstances.

***

What holds you secure when your snow globe is shaken?

What scripture do you turn to that reassures you of God's presence in your life?

When have you felt a peace that passes all understanding?

Even if...

Father God, lead me where my trust is without boundaries. Help me trust You even when my prayers go unanswered, and help me not lean on my own understanding. Amen.

Trust sounds easy enough until life takes you to a place you never imagined, a place where the water is murky and you fear that taking a step forward may land you in quicksand, with no idea how you are going to get out.

Trust is hard when a diagnosis you didn't see coming hits you in the gut and in the mind. So many questions. How did this happen? What will the next few months look like? What if... nope, not going there.

It's one thing to live with a life-threatening diagnosis; it's another to walk beside someone who has just been given one. Having walked with a dear friend through the valley of cancer, I know all too well how scary the future can look.

The **what-ifs** are scary. What if God doesn't answer our prayers? What if the valley of the shadow of death is real? What if I do fear evil? What then? This is where Faith, or our lack of it, becomes real. This is where our conversations with God take a different direction. I've had a few conversations with God that haven't been "church lady" nice. I wasn't turned into a pillar of salt or a vapor. God led me straight to the Scriptures and reminded me He would never leave me, no matter how angry I got with Him and told Him, "God, this isn't fair!"

There are moments in life when it feels as if the Big Bad Wolf is at my front door and the Grinch is at the back door. Both are after my Faith and me. They know my weaknesses.

I had to decide whether to believe the Scriptures and that God loves my friend and me, or to walk away from my Faith. I chose Faith.

> Even though I walk through the darkest valley, I will fear no evil, for you are with me; your rod and your staff, comfort me. (Psalm 23:4)

Walking the cancer journey with my friend taught me a lot about my Faith. One afternoon, Barb, her sister, Kathy, and I were chatting in Barb's hospital room. Barb's favorite nurse, Kim, came in to check the chemo IV. She had heard that we sang in a Gospel Trio, The Three of His, for over thirty years. She asked us to sing. I suggested she shut the door. "Oh no," she said. "The other patients and the nursing staff need to hear you."

We sang "Because He Lives."

The song echoed down the hallway, to the nurse's desk, and into the rooms of other patients. For a few moments, the cruelty of cancer was softened.

Copyright laws don't allow me to quote the lyrics, so if you don't know the song, please Google "Because He Lives." Knowing who holds our future gives us the strength to face tomorrow. Because of Jesus, life will always be worth living.

Bill and Gloria Gaither wrote "Because He Lives" in 1971. There is no way they could have known the impact the song would still have over fifty years later.

That afternoon, many tears were wiped away on the sixth floor of St. Vincent Hospital in Indianapolis, Indiana. It was July 2025. Only a few weeks had passed since Barb was diagnosed with acute myeloid leukemia.

Barb lost her battle with leukemia a few weeks later.

God didn't answer our prayers, but we have the promise of Heaven.

Barb told me that when she got better, she was considering getting a tattoo on her wrist that said ***Even if.*** She believed God is a good God, even if He didn't answer her prayers. She never had a chance to get her tattoo. Her son, Eric, says he will get it for her.

I had the honor of speaking at her Celebration of Life. Barb lived her life as if acts of kindness made the world a better place. The hundreds who stood in line at the funeral home shared stories of her kindness, showing that what she believed about kindness was true.

We were all changed for the better because we knew Barb. I loved what her cousin, Jim McGee, said during his eulogy for her: "We don't age because of time, but of the stories we live—stories of joy, sadness, anticipation, hopefulness, and celebration."

I pray we can all learn from Barb's life and from the trust she had in God.

She will have no fear of bad news; her heart is steadfast, trusting in her Lord. (Psalm 112:7, adapted)

The voice of Barb's Faith was louder than the voice of her fear.

As Jim McGee closed in prayer at the gravesite, he said these words, "Grief is love's unwillingness to let go, but Faith is love's assurance that it never has to."

I will continue to pray the prayer I prayed at the beginning of this chapter. My heart knows the words well.

***

Have you ever walked a journey with someone who has been given a life-threatening illness?

How did you both navigate it?

What did you learn about your Faith and about yourself?

The Affirmations

Never tell God you will never do something.

And so, in the summer of 2024, as I was sitting at a She Speaks Conference in Charlotte, North Carolina, I noticed the Christian speaker had something on her forearm. No way… yes, it was a tattoo.

I immediately thought, "I could never do that."

While I have never heard the voice of God audibly, I have heard Him in my spirit. I heard, "Do you want to be a safe witness for me or a brave one?"

I squirmed in my seat as I considered what people would think of me if I, a Christian writer and speaker, got a tattoo. What would my family think? I already knew: *She's lost her mind.*

As I sat there, trying to listen to the speaker, I thought about the scripture God gave me some twenty years earlier, when I started selling cars and trucks, a vocation I never imagined pursuing.

> For I am going to do something in your days that you would
> not believe, even if you were told. (Habakkuk 1:5)

I have no idea what the speaker said that day, but I do know that God said, "Be a brave witness for me."

I remember praying, "Father, God, I need an affirmation."

Affirmation #1

A few weeks later, I was on a tour of historic homes in my town. At one home, I recognized a woman I hadn't seen in many years, Megan. I noticed her tattoo and asked her to tell me about it. It was in honor of her sister, who had passed away. She told me who did it. I told her I was thinking about getting one and what I wanted it to say. She said, "Do it!" She thought it would be a great witness to my Faith.

Even after my conversation with Megan, I started arguing with God. I was almost seventy years old. I was a Christian writer and speaker. I grew up (and grew old) with the idea that tattoos were not something Christian ladies had on their bodies. I even cited Leviticus 19:28, where God told Moses to tell the people not to put tattoo marks on their bodies. Who argues with God using a Scripture reference?

I asked God for another affirmation.

Affirmation #2

A few weeks later, my best friend, Patrice, and I were sitting at Grindstone Public House, a restaurant downtown. I noticed our server had a sleeve tattoo. If you are not familiar with it, a sleeve tattoo is a collection of meaningful tattoos on an arm. When I asked her about it, she said, "Well, it started with a Scripture verse." I almost choked on my onion ring. I had not told my bestie until that moment what I was thinking of doing. Of course, she laughed. She knows me as well as anyone. A tattoo and Janet are not something anyone would put into fruition. Then Patrice said, "Do it."

Affirmation #3

As I walked home, I passed the tattoo parlor where Megan went for her tattoo. I'd researched the artist she mentioned. After all, I research and Google everything before buying a new appliance, let alone getting a tattoo.

I knew what the guy looked like. There he was, sitting outside the parlor on a bench, taking a break. I asked him if he was Chris. He said, "Maybe."

I explained my thoughts and my fears. He told me he was raised by his Christian grandmother in the Baptist church. He loved tattooing scripture onto his clients. He said it would be an awesome witness. He also said it would be an honor for him to be the one to give me a tattoo. I told him to stay tuned, as I was still praying about it.

Affirmation #4

Somewhere in the midst of all this, I asked my husband what he thought. He smiled and said, "Janet, I'd be proud to tell my friends that my wife has a tattoo."

When I told my daughter, Emily, and my daughter-in-love, Angie, what I was thinking about doing, they both thought I was crazy and having a midlife crisis. I don't think I'll live to be 140. I don't think they thought I'd ever follow through with it. I proved them wrong.

So, in October 2024, I bravely walked into Mystic Images Tattoos and held out my forearm, telling Chris, "Let's do this!" I pleaded with him not to misspell Habakkuk and to use a font that wouldn't look wrinkly as I aged.

Affirmation #5 (After the fact)

A few weeks later, I was on a plane returning home from Tampa. The woman next to me noticed my forearm tattoo. As I explained it, I saw tears well in her eyes. She said she was going through a hard time. She had never heard of Habakkuk and had not opened her Bible in many years. She said, "When I get home, I will be opening my Bible."

I have other stories about how my tattoo has become a visual witness for God's Word to complete strangers.

Maybe I am crazy. Maybe I am brave. I just know I have five affirmations God gave me, and a forearm that bears witness to the fact that God does things no one would believe even if they were told.

See, I have engraved you on the palms of my hands. (Isaiah 49:16)

***

When have you felt God telling you to do something?

When have you argued with God?

How did it change how you feel about God truly seeing you?

When God Gives You a Dream

You can't say that. But I did.

You can't do that. But I did.

You are too old. Apparently, I'm not.

You are not smart enough. Apparently, I am.

You are a female. And that decides what I can do?

You aren't enough. But God says I am.

Never doubt the dream God has placed in your heart.

While most of this pertains to my writing, it also relates to many of the decisions I have made in my life.

As a little girl, I dreamed of writing a book someday, but dropping out of college and reaching my 60s wiped out that dream, or so I thought.

For almost twenty years, I have written a newspaper column. For those of you who have not read my first book, *When the Hart Speaks,* you should know that the first column I wrote was the result of a dare. I told my friend Jay, who dared me, all the reasons I could not write a column. Those reasons were debunked, and within a few weeks of my submission, I became a weekly columnist for the local newspaper. Who knew that the *Noblesville Ledger's* call for guest columnists would lead to my becoming one for twenty years?

Some of the columns I have written took more gumption than I ever thought I could muster. I learned that it's okay to be afraid, as long as we are doing something we know we must do. When God laid on my heart what I needed to say, I had to stop worrying about what people would think.

I often shake my head as I think about being a lifelong people-pleaser and a worrier about what people think of me, and then write a newspaper column sharing my opinions. I'm a sitting target on the front page of the *Hamilton County Reporter* every Monday, which makes me an easy target for criticism. Sadly, the *Noblesville Ledger* is no longer being published, but Don Jellison brought me to the *Hamilton County Reporter* in 2014. Stu, Isaac, Paul, and Ray are brave owners who allow me to share my thoughts and my Faith.

I've had my share of criticism, but I've had even more "atta girl" affirmations. I receive emails that say, "Me too" and "You said exactly how I feel." My love language is words of affirmation, so these words hug my heart.

I don't take for granted that I have a voice in the local newspaper. It is an honor and a calling.

Finding my calling has been a lifelong process. My calling has looked different as I've gotten older and as life has changed me. I find myself in a different place with different experiences. I've learned not to say, "I'd never think that way, say that, or feel that way." What I've survived has shaped my thoughts and opinions.

Wisdom can be found after making both good and bad decisions, but especially after the bad ones. Life's detours lead us through dark, scary valleys, yet eventually we realize we are where we were meant to be all along. We may look a little bruised and broken, but we can carry a sign that says, "What the enemy meant for my harm, God meant for my good." This comes from the story of Joseph in Genesis 50:20.

When I was in high school, I remember kneeling at the altar of that little Nazarene Church. I prayed for God to use me to make a difference in the world. I heard the words echo in my heart: "You watch, you wait, and you will see."

For many years, I waited. As I grew older, I honestly thought my days of influence were behind me. I hit every major disqualification. Lack of a college degree. Divorce. Fear of using my voice. Age. And yes, even being female.

The voices in my head gave me excuse after excuse as to why I had lost my calling.

Then one day I pictured God saying, "Janet, hold My wine cup while I show you how I work in strange and mysterious ways."

One of my favorite New Testament stories is in Mark 6, where Jesus fed 5,000 people with five loaves of bread and two fish. In the story, a little boy offered everything he had to Jesus.

There wasn't enough food to feed 5,000 people until Jesus took the bread and fish and blessed them. But look what Jesus did. He can take the gifts we have and do far more than we could ever do.

> Now to him who is able to do immeasurably more than all we
> ask or imagine, according to his power that is at work within
> us. (Ephesians 3:20)

When you begin to believe and to see what God has done in your life, your Faith grows. I am not a believer in happenstance but in Divine Intervention and Blessed Appointments.

I often say that God doesn't call the qualified but qualifies the called.

I only know that God gave a voice to a woman who didn't have a college degree, felt she was too old, and didn't believe she was qualified.

My prayer is that I can use my voice to show my readers who God can be in their lives. I know who He has been in mine.

It's my story for His glory as I write book #2, *From the Hart*.

> I have become a sign to many; you are my strong refuge.
> (Psalm 71:7)

***

What have you done even though you were afraid?

How did it make you feel?

How did it change you?

Sustaining Grace

I hung up the phone. It was back when phones were mounted on the kitchen wall. It was harvest gold to match the colors in my kitchen. It was the mid-1990s.

I can still remember the yellow wallpaper and its design. I can still hear the caller's words vividly. Her words plunged me into a world of disbelief, anxiety, and heartache.

Life as I knew it was turned upside down. The prayers I prayed felt like they were knocking on a locked door, and God wasn't answering. The Bible verses I memorized as a child felt like clanging cymbals. This was the greatest test of my Faith. I had no idea how I would get through this nightmare.

How do you pray yourself out of a nightmare?

Do you know how it feels to count the ceiling tiles in a therapist's office to avoid making eye contact? Do you know how it feels to walk into a place where you feel the eyes of those in the room are not just watching you but judging you? Do you know how it feels, some thirty years later, to feel those feelings as if they were happening today?

I always thought that if I prayed hard enough, studied my Bible, and was a good Christian girl, my prayers would always be answered. My goodness, how naive I was!

Being judged was like pouring salt into my ever-so-tender heart. If I had been a better… If I had done more… If I had done things differently. I questioned my decisions, and if I'm being honest, I questioned my Faith.

Other people didn't go to church, and they seemed to be living footloose and fancy-free. I was living on a prayer that was going nowhere.

And then came Grace—Sustaining Grace: the ongoing divine strength and support that empowers individuals to persevere through life's challenges.

> My grace is sufficient for you, for my power is made perfect
> in weakness. (2 Corinthians 12:9)

All of a sudden, people started showing up in my life who would carry me through the hard days. Think what you want, but I know God knew I needed them. They had walked the same hard journey. They knew the words I needed to hear.

I began searching the Scriptures like never before. I found promises in the Bible I had never noticed. I began marking in my Bible the date and the promise of each scripture. I started praying for more of Jesus in my life. "Shout to the Lord" by Hillsong Worship became my battle cry. At times, I could only lift my hands and wipe away tears as I listened to the words.

Most of the time, we are taught about Hebrews 11 and how it is the Faith chapter, but I found scriptural gold in Hebrews 10.

Let us hold unswervingly to the hope we profess, for he who promised is faithful. (Hebrews 10:23)

As I read a bit further...

Remember those earlier days after you had received the light, when you endured in a great conflict full of suffering. (Hebrews 10:32)

So do not throw away your confidence; it will be richly rewarded. You need to persevere so that when you have done the will of God, you will receive what he has promised. (Hebrews 10:35-36)

I claimed those verses, and they carried me through some really dark valleys. Yes, more than one.

Did God answer my prayers the way I asked? The answer is no, but His Sustaining Grace carried me and gave me the strength to persevere.

It was during that time that I realized what my Faith truly looked like. Now, almost thirty years later, my Faith rests on the foundation of the Scriptures and the faithfulness of God.

I'll never forget the day I answered that harvest gold phone, and my Faith was tested far beyond what I ever imagined.

***

When have you been faced with something so difficult that you questioned your Faith?

How did you navigate and overcome discouragement?

What scripture has become a lifeline for you during difficult times?

But I Have the Right to be Angry

Have you ever been madder than an old wet hen? Have you ever wanted to jerk a knot in someone's tail? Have you ever had to remind yourself that you are a nice Christian lady and should not show anger?

Even when I ask those questions and remember when someone I love was hurt, I feel what I call righteous indignation stir within me. Indignation is anger aroused by something unjust or mean.

This is where my journaling comes in. Writing my feelings in a journal is my therapy. Then I pray and study the Scriptures. Often, I am amazed at how the Scriptures speak to my emotions.

While fighting the urge to use my keyboard to voice my not-so-nice thoughts, I open my Bible to the Psalms. It is my go-to Old Testament book when I am feeling emotionally negative. Angry. Fit to be tied. In a tizzy. You get the idea.

> Truly my soul finds rest in God; my salvation comes from
> him. Truly he is my rock and my salvation; he is my fortress,
> I will never be shaken. (Psalm 62:1-2)

It's like a voice from Heaven saying, "See, Janet, I've got this!" I may not understand the behind-the-scenes workings of God, but when I read a scripture that speaks to my heart, I can't help but do the Happy Day Hallelujah Dance. This dance celebrates the fact that God sees me.

I underline the scripture in my Bible. Then I write the date beside it and scribble a note about what was going on at the time. My Bible has become a sort of diary/journal. I've done this for over twenty-five years.

I've actually worn out one Bible. Many pages are no longer attached to the binding. The book of Ruth was cut out when my granddaughter, Alecksa, got hold of the scissors at age three. She is now twenty-eight.

Some may look at that tattered, pitiful-looking Bible and want to toss it, but to me it is a treasure. It has a story to tell. I hope my daughter, Emily, finds it after my death and takes the time to look through it. It's my story, a story of pain and redemption. It's the history of my spiritual journey and of how God held my pen as He wrote my story.

I am in awe of how relevant Scripture remains today, many years after it was written. I'm even more in awe of how God directs my heart to the exact verses I need to read. Don't ever tell me that God isn't in the details.

As I read through Psalm 62, I come to the part that talks about the enemy, aka satan, trying to topple me. It says that my enemy sees me as a broken-down wall or a tottering fence. The enemy uses others to wear me down, make me angrier than an old wet hen, and give me the desire to jerk a knot in someone's tail.

But... oh, how I love the word, but,

> My salvation and my honor depend on God; he is my mighty
> rock, my refuge. (Psalm 62:7)

While reading Psalm 62, I envision the enemy holding a large mallet, with me as the little mole in whack-a-mole. In many ways, he is trying to bring issues into my life and the lives of those I care about. The enemy seeks to wear me down and lead me into the valley of discouragement. Nope, not going there. Ain't going to happen. Whack. He missed me again.

> Yes, my soul, find rest in God; my hope comes from him.
> (Psalm 62:5)

It isn't easy to wait quietly, especially when I am angry or worried. I want to see justice, ASAP. I want all the worrisome ends tied up in a pretty bow. It happens in Hallmark movies, but certainly not in real life. I admit it may take a few days to settle down. I need time to ponder the Scriptures and pray.

As I am writing this, I remember a song by Phil Wickham. I open YouTube and listen to "The Battle Belongs to You."

I've learned to fight my battles on my knees. I lift my hands as I worship the God who truly sees and gives me strength and clarity. God sees my hurt, my anger, and my worries.

Again, you can't tell me that God isn't in the details. I have the scriptures and the songs to prove it.

You might notice that I do not capitalize satan. Grammarly tells me I should, but I'm not giving the enemy any recognition, importance, or power.

I'm just sitting here quietly, waiting for the victory. I let my loved ones know that we will see it, and God will get the Glory... my Bible tells me so.

***

When have you been so angry because of an injustice that you wanted to say something you knew you would regret?

How did you handle it?

How difficult is it to allow God to fight your battles?

Empty-Heart Syndrome

It's the silence. It is so loud that it's deafening.

It was twenty-seven years ago, yet I remember it as if it were yesterday. Emily and I drove the two hours and six minutes to Indiana State University in Terre Haute. Yes, I counted the minutes. We arrived there so quickly that day, and it felt just as quick as all the years Emily was growing up.

We carried the totes, baskets, and clothes on hangers into the dorm. I didn't have time to think about the empty room and closet I'd see when I got back home. I made the bed, which was tucked snugly into the corner of her dorm room. What about the bed at home that wouldn't need to be made for weeks?

We drove to Walmart to pick up a few things she still needed. Have I taught her everything she will need to know? Does she remember how to separate clothes, so she doesn't end up with a shrunken blouse I paid too much for? Does she remember that Fels-Naptha is the best stain remover? Have I taught her how to survive on her own? Trouble is, no one has taught me how to live without her daily presence.

Does she know how much I need her? I covered my aching heart with chatter and laughter. "Emily, you've got this! How fun this is going to be!" I told myself I've got this. I was lying.

The drive back home seemed to take hours. I had trouble taking a deep breath. My chest felt as if a thousand memories were lying on it.

I walked inside the back door, and I heard it. It was so loud. It was loudly quiet.

That was twenty-seven years ago, yet I remember. Oh, how I remember.

Fast forward to now.

Emily calls me. She is washing the football uniform of soon-to-be-fifteen-year-old Aiden. She tells me she is scrubbing it with Fels-Naptha. I have to laugh. I taught her well. She remembered.

In four years, she will take Aiden to college. She will understand how I felt all those years ago when I drove her to Indiana State University. Should I tell her how fast it will go? Should I tell her to grab every chance for a hug, even if he shrugs it off a bit? Should I tell her that the forty-five-minute drive to Tampa Jesuit every morning will give her the chance to equip him with encouraging words, advice, and priceless time together? Yes, the time spent driving in Tampa traffic will be brutal, but in four years, she will treasure it—even the silent moments when he is asleep.

I need to tell her to embrace and pack in those fun yet exhausting moments of high school. Take a gazillion pictures, even the ones where he won't be serious.

Here's another thing I need to tell her. Those kids who call you "Mama" and look nothing like you? You will still be their "other" mother when they are grown. How do I know? I still get called Mama Janet all these years later.

I will forever keep track of my redheaded daughter, Sarah, from another mother. I follow sweet Renee on social media, who spent many a night at our house. And of course, your best friend since you were two, Angie, who became your sister-in-law and is like a daughter to me. I still love them and pray for them. You will do the same with Aiden's friends.

This will happen again with Leah, who is two years younger than Aiden. It doesn't get easier with each child. It hits differently. It's one of the most challenging aspects of being a parent. You are not told how hard it will be when your nest is empty.

Your house will be less messy. Your refrigerator will be full. You will have to learn to cook less food. You will mark your calendar for the times when all your kids will be home. Each time they leave, you will have recurring episodes of Empty-Heart Syndrome.

Empty-Heart Syndrome is a real thing.

Every time Emily and I talk about the day I took her to ISU, she remembers the day after, when she came to Riverview Hospital to visit me. You see, after I got home from dropping her off, the chest pains worsened, and I was admitted to the hospital with chest pain, triggered by an anxiety attack. Acute Empty-Heart Syndrome was my unofficial diagnosis.

All you mamas out there who are hurting, I see you. I know your pain, and you may not believe me, but it will get better. Just know that the pain comes back if they move 988 miles away, as my daughter did. My heart knows exactly how many miles she moved away. Believe it or not, I'm okay. It just took time. Once I saw her so happy, I realized that was all that mattered.

I need to interject an important fact here. I still feel a twinge of Empty-Heart Syndrome whenever I hug Emily and say, "See you later" at the airport.

***

Are you an Empty-Heart Syndrome survivor, or is your nest still full?

How did you deal with it, or think you will deal with it?

Do the feelings reoccur when you have to say goodbye, even today?

It Takes a Village

For the May 2025 Mother's Day column in the Hamilton County Reporter, I handed the keyboard to my daughter, Emily Catron Alexander. Here are her thoughts.

When people say, "It takes a village to raise a child," it's not about a parent's limitations. In our home, it means weaving a vibrant community that pours love, support, and wisdom into our children's lives. This village shapes who our kids become, molding their values, dreams, and hearts. As we celebrate Mother's Day, I'm reflecting on the incredible role this community plays—not just for my children, but for me and countless others. I'm filled with gratitude for the woman who showed me how to build it: my mom.

With our kids' whirlwind schedules—sports, school, and everything in between—our village is a lifeline. We lean on grandparents, friends, coaches, and neighbors to keep things running smoothly. I sometimes feel guilty about relying on them so much, but then I realize: I'm part of someone else's village, too. When I cheer for our kids' friends at their games, offer a ride, or lend a listening ear, I don't hesitate. It's an honor. Mother's Day reminds me that this mutual support is the heartbeat of our villages, and I'm so grateful to everyone who steps up.

Growing up, my parents surrounded me with an incredible village, and I'm especially thankful for the "bonus moms" who loved me like their own. These women offered guidance, encouragement, and unwavering support, and even now, they're still there for me, no matter how much time has passed. I've also heard from childhood friends who share how my mom touched their lives, becoming a beacon of light in their villages. This Mother's Day, I'm celebrating these women who showed me what it means to mother beyond their children, and I owe so much of that understanding to my mom's example.

As my kids have grown, I've noticed their friends moving from calling me "Aiden and Leah's mom" to "Momma Emily" or their "second mom." It's a title that humbles me and fills me with pride. I now understand the privilege of being a trusted figure in their lives, just as those bonus moms were for me. Mother's Day is the perfect time to honor this role—to celebrate the joy of offering love and support to the kids who call me their second mom, and to every mother figure who steps into that sacred space for others.

A special thanks goes to my mom, who loved us so well and taught me what it means to be a mom and a bonus mom. Her fierce love, endless patience, and open heart showed me how to nurture my children and extend that care to others. She didn't just raise me; she modeled how to build a village, love beyond family lines, and be a light for someone else's child. This Mother's Day, I'm celebrating her and the legacy of love she's passed down.

My deepest hope as a mother has always been to surround my children with a community that loves and uplifts them, no matter what. Now I also pray to be a positive influence on their friends and to be a bonus mom or a steady presence in their villages, just as my mom was and is. This Mother's Day, I'm celebrating not just biological moms but every person who mothers—grandmas, aunts, neighbors, teachers, friends, and especially my incredible mom—all of whom make our villages so strong. Here's to the love we share, the communities we build, and the countless ways we show up for each other's children.

Happy Mother's Day to every heart that helps raise a child.

***

What is something you learned from your mom and are passing on to your children?

As a child, did you have a bonus mom?

Are you a bonus mom to any of your children's friends?

Originally published in the Hamilton County Reporter, May 11, 2025. Reprinted with permission.

Could I Have This Dance

In January 2014, Chuck and I walked into the Hamilton County Judicial Center to apply for our marriage license. Chuck was seventy-four, and I was fifty-eight.

I wondered why one needed a license to get married. Of course, I asked Google.

A marriage license confirms that a person is legally eligible to marry, verifying that they are not already married to anyone else, are not closely related, and meet the age requirements. We checked all the boxes.

Our ages should tell the powers that be that we knew what we were doing. Chuck was happily married for fifty-one years before his wife, Nancy, passed away from cancer. I was married for twenty-four years, eleven months, and five days before I signed the "he doesn't love you anymore" papers. I had been single for fourteen years.

We both had broken hearts. Then our hearts met.

Love feels different at fifty-eight and seventy-four. Love should be a soft place to fall, a place of trust and security. Our past relationships give us a deeper understanding of what love truly is. We appreciate the tenderness of a love where patience is paramount. If history has taught us anything, it is to love well and to live in the moment.

We danced... and I knew. I wanted Chuck to be my partner every night. It felt right, and I wanted to dance with him for the rest of my life. Those moments were magical. He was all I would ever need. Oh, Anne Murray, you sang it well.

I waited fourteen years. He was the man God knew I needed. He always smiles when I tell him he was and is the answer to my prayers—actually, above and beyond what I asked for.

> God can do anything, you know—far more than you could ever imagine or guess or request in your wildest dreams. (Ephesians 3:20 MSG)

God gave me that promise long before I met Chuck.

Most mornings, we can be found at our kitchen table. We sit catty-corner from each other, sipping our coffee. I'm usually on my second cup because I rise early to have my devotions and write. If I'm not going anywhere that day, I change into my writing pajamas, which are a bit dressier than the ones I sleep in.

Chuck reads the *Indianapolis Star* and does the crossword puzzle. He amazes me with his word knowledge. I seem to amaze him with my Janetisms. A Janetism is a phrase or word not found in a dictionary. Some of them I inherited from my mother. Audreyisms are fascinating words that make total sense when explained.

Chuck has always seemed to enjoy my cooking, which is mostly Southern comfort food. But he refuses to try my chocolate gravy over biscuits. I've included the recipe, along with a few others, in this book.

We make each other laugh. Like the time I found out he rearranges the dishwasher after I load it. Sometimes, I might refold the towels and his whites after he folds them. He notices, and then we laugh.

On occasion, I make "suggestions" about his driving. It's more like a sound or a way of trying to press the invisible brake on my side of the car. I know how much he "appreciates" my help. You know I wrote that with a bit of sarcasm. I say to Chuck as I put my hand on his, "I'm just trying to be a blessing." He says, "Oh, I'm blessed, alright." And we laugh. Then he sings, "Count Your Blessings."

There is no one else I would rather have in my life to drive me crazy. There is no one else I would rather have sitting catty-corner to me at the kitchen table. And there is no one else I'd rather dance with for the rest of my life.

***

What parts of your love story do you want your children and grandchildren to know? How might you preserve those memories for them?

What song instantly brings back memories of someone you love?

How do you "bless" your husband with your driving advice?

She

She sits quietly at her kitchen table. Her fingers wrap around her coffee cup. She stares out the window and ponders, "Is it enough?" Will what she has to say reach her readers' minds and touch their hearts? Will her words make a difference? She never wants to come across as preachy or judgmental. The world has enough of that.

And still she writes. She bows her head and prays, "Father God, give me the words—not to bring them to church, but to You."

Her prayer is simple. She's not a preacher. She's not a theologian. She's not a Bible study teacher. She's simply a woman who loves her Lord, and she's been given the gift of words and the honor of sharing them. She does not take that lightly. The weight of her words weighs heavily on her heart as she writes.

May her words be soft and gentle as she tells her readers that things will be okay... eventually. She knows this well. She hopes she has paid enough dues to spare others from having to pay them. May they learn from her mistakes, so they do not have to suffer the same consequences.

She prays that they are given a glimpse of a miracle, and when circumstances make it hard to pray, may they find strength to whisper, "Thy will be done." May they be given a glimmer of hope when nothing makes sense and they live in a fog of discouragement. She knows how they feel. She's lived it.

May her words be a soft place to fall, offering comfort to those whose pain reaches the very depths of their hearts—a place where love for their family lives. She hopes her family knows how much she loves them, even when they are far away.

She knows, as she has entered the winter of her life, that her days will decrease in the amount of time she has left to write the words God has laid on her heart. She hopes that someday, after she has taken her last breath, it can be said,

> The Lord fulfilled His purpose for her. (Psalm 138:8, ESV, adapted)

Even as her light grows dim, may it continue to shine and lead others to Jesus. Prayers are not just words to her; they are deep longings spoken to her Savior with the confidence that He hears and works all things for her good and for God's purpose. She may not see it while she is here on Earth, but she knows Heaven sees things from a different perspective.

She believes that, even as she continues to endure hard times, Scripture will always reassure her of God's love for her.

> I remain confident of this: I will see the goodness of the Lord
> in the land of the living. Wait for the Lord; be strong and take
> heart and wait for the Lord. (Psalm 27:13-14)

She sees in Scripture that she is told *twice* to wait. Those words tell her that the wait may be long, but she will learn to trust God in it. It is there she will find peace, *not* after her prayers are answered, but in the waiting. It's a calming assurance to know she can find goodness in the waiting.

She has told her family that she wants the song "The Goodness of God" sung at her Celebration of Life. God has been faithful, and He has shown her so much goodness. His mercies have not failed her. The Scriptures have been her lifeline during times of depression and failure, when she struggled to see the goodness. Eventually, it was there.

She found that she could sing "It Is Well with My Soul," even when things in her life were not well.

So much goodness was found, even though she felt the enemy had stolen so much from her.

She looks at the messiness of her Bible. She has underlined and highlighted the scriptures that kept her going. They seemed to be exactly what she needed to read at the time. Those highlights told her she was seen by God. In Hebrew, *El Roi* means "the God who sees."

People often look for heroes, but she wonders if they can be found in a praying mother or grandmother.

She writes from her heart. She is a storyteller. She hopes her words land softly in her readers' hearts. She hopes that someday people will say, "Her words mattered." And so, she continues to write.

My Final Thoughts... for now

How do you know a book is finished? It certainly isn't when the author has run out of words, because we never do. You just have to finally stop and remember that there is always another book to be written.

This book has been a work in progress for quite some time, yet it came together in January 2026 during an epic snowstorm. Here in central Indiana, ten to twelve inches of snowfall and a wind chill below zero have kept this author inside the house. It seems the words were no longer stuck in molasses but flowed like melted butter.

I discovered something I never thought about before... writing pajamas! Every morning, around 5:00, I changed out of my sleeping pajamas into writing pajamas. They were a bit dressy, made of a rich, silky material with a deep fuchsia, blue, or gold design. I put on earrings and a bit of makeup and headed to the kitchen table. Who knew writing pajamas would be a thing? Don't think for a moment they were expensive. I'm a TJ Maxx kind of girl.

I sipped my coffee, sweetened with Chobani Sweet Cream and topped with Sweet Cream foam. I do like my coffee sweet. I lit a candle and went into author mode. As the snow fell and the temperatures dropped, I decided to stay put. For a few days, most places were closed, and travel was forbidden. As I told Chuck, at our age, if we fall and break something, it may not be repairable. However, I did sneak out and shovel a few times. I have always loved to shovel the snow.

I hope you enjoyed my words and that they gave you something to ponder. I hope you found the questions at the end of each chapter enjoyable to answer.

Where do I go from here?

There are, of course, more words to be written, including my weekly newspaper column, another book of my thoughts, and possibly a fiction book. My little mind has a story to tell about a hairdresser named Audrey Grace who wasn't a preacher or an attorney, but who held many secrets back in 1989 in the hills of Kentucky in a tiny town called Sunny Gap. A new preacher arrives to serve at the little Baptist church. He's not a nice man, and he might just go missing, and the plot thickens.

Chuck and I have more dances to dance, more coffee to drink, and more time at our kitchen table, where we share our days. I still cross my heart and promise to give him all the love I have to give.

I hope my thoughts have warmed your hearts, made you smile, and perhaps made you think.

I hope you, too, can use your voice to make our world a bit kinder and less ugly. I ask you to open your mind, your heart, and maybe your kitchen table to those who are different from you.

I hope you can shut out the loud voices and hear, in your heart, what God has to say to you. There is strength to be found in the quiet of your day. Seek and find who God can be in your life.

Psalm 71 was one of my mother's favorites. It was how she lived her life so that her family and all who knew her would come to know her God. I hope I've become like my mother.

> Since my youth, God, you have taught me, and to this day I declare your marvelous deeds. Even when I am old and gray, do not forsake me, my God, till I declare your power to the next generation, your mighty acts to all who are to come. (Psalm 71:18)

I have no idea how far this book will reach and who will read it, but I do know you've all been prayed for—every last one of you.

That young girl who heard, in her spirit, the words, "You watch, you wait, and you will see," is still hearing them today.

Thank you all for taking the time to read my thoughts. I hope you felt the gentle hug that came with my thoughts.

Blessings,

Janet

Janet's Southern Comfort Recipes

I promised there would be a few of my favorite family recipes tucked in this book. If you ever sit at my kitchen table, there is a good chance you will be fed. I was raised on comfort food where calories are devoured, not counted. I could easily write a cookbook, but these are a few of my favorite things to cook and bake. I hope you enjoy these recipes.

Chocolate Gravy

Chocolate Gravy is a Southern comfort recipe from my Kentucky family. It can be served any time of day, but I had it for breakfast as a child. All my cousins still make it for their families.

¾ c white sugar
3 tbsp all-purpose flour
¼ c Hershey's cocoa powder

Whisk in a saucepan until no lumps remain.
Slowly add 2 c of milk (whole or 2%)
Whisk until there are no lumps.
Stir over medium heat, 7–10 minutes, until it thickens to a gravy consistency.
Remove from heat.

Add:
1 tsp butter (Don't you dare use margarine)
2 tsp vanilla extract

Serve over hot biscuits with a dab of butter. ENJOY!

Fruit Cocktail Cake

I also call this Funeral Cake because my mother always made it for the church dinner when someone passed away. Do not count the calories. So much of my mother's legacy is found in my kitchen as I prepare the recipes that were a huge part of my growing up.

Preheat oven to 350°F.

2 c all-purpose flour
2 tsp baking soda
½ tsp salt
2 eggs
1 ½ c sugar
1 can (15 oz) fruit cocktail in heavy syrup

Stir together. Pour into a 9x12-inch pan.
Mix ½ c pecans and ½ c brown sugar.
Sprinkle over batter.
Bake for 45 minutes

Icing:
2 sticks butter
1½ c sugar
½ c pecans
½ c coconut
1 c evaporated milk

Cook for 1 minute after it starts to boil.

Pour over the cake while it is still warm.

Sugar Cream Pie

This is the Indiana State Pie. For our family dinners, I have to make several so they have some to take home. For me, nothing tells my family how much I love them as cooking does.

Preheat oven to 375°F.

Make a pie crust or thaw one from the freezer. I prefer Marie Callendar's Deep Dish Pie Crust.
Do not bake the pie shell.

Combine in a saucepan:
¾ c white sugar
1/8 tsp salt
2 c half-and-half
½ c whipping cream

Bring to a boil.

While the cream mixture heats, in another saucepan, combine:
¼ c brown sugar
¼ c cornstarch

Gradually whisk the hot mixture into the brown sugar mixture.
Add ½ c butter (DO NOT use margarine).
Cook over medium heat, whisking constantly, for 5 minutes, or until thick.
Simmer 1 minute. Remove from heat and add 1 tsp vanilla.
Pour into unbaked pie shell and lightly sprinkle with cinnamon and nutmeg.

Bake for 25 minutes.

Taco Stew

This is my go-to comfort food, whether it's just Chuck and me or a gathering of family and friends. Just add more ingredients if needed. Leftover stew can be frozen.

Brown 1½ lbs ground beef in a Dutch oven or stew pot.
Drain the beef and add it back into the pot.

Add:
1 46-oz can of tomato juice
1 15-oz can black beans (drained)
1 15-oz can dark red beans (drained)
1 15-oz can southwest corn (drained)
1 15-oz can petite diced tomatoes
1 package taco seasoning (mild or spicy)

I divide the stew into two pots because I like it mild, and my husband likes it spicy.

Let it simmer for at least an hour. It will thicken the longer you cook it. I often make it the day before, so the ingredients have time to "stew." I then add a bit more tomato juice as it thickens.

When you are ready to eat, pour into bowls and top with Mexican cheese, sour cream, and Fritos.

Yummy Salad

This will be quite different from most salads you've eaten. It's a meal in itself. Once you make it, it will become a recipe you make again and again. Trust me, it's that delicious.

SALAD

1 package spring mix greens

3 c chopped broccoli

1 medium red onion, thinly sliced

1 can of mandarin oranges, drained

Mix everything and set aside while you make the dressing and crunchies.

DRESSING

½ c canola oil

½ c sugar

¼ c red wine vinegar

2 tbsp soy sauce

Mix all ingredients. The dressing can be refrigerated for up to a week. Stir well before adding to salad.

CRUNCHIES

2 packages ramen noodles (discard the seasoning packets)
Break up the noodles into very small pieces. (I use a meat mallet to break up the noodles while still in packages.)

Sauté the ramen noodles in 1 stick of butter.

When noodles are just starting to brown, add 1 c chopped pecans and heat through.

Add crunchies and dressing to the salad and toss before serving.

JANET HART LEONARD is an award-winning columnist and bestselling author who brings Scripture to life with humor, heart, and a gift for storytelling. For over two decades, her beloved weekly column, "From the Hart," has appeared in various local newspapers, where readers have come to cherish her kitchen-table wisdom and tender-hearted voice.

Known for her wit and whimsical wisdom, Janet encourages women to believe that God isn't done with their story. He's crafting a Greatest Hits Album, not a one-hit wonder. Her messages, rooted in grace and real-life experience, invite others to find joy even in unfair seasons and to discover that it's never too late for God to do something beautiful.

Janet is the author of *When the Hart Speaks: Whimsy and Wisdom from the Little House on the Alley* and a contributing author to the bestselling anthologies *Strength in the Storm* (Silver Selah Award winner) and *Successful in His Eyes*. *From the Hart* is her second solo book, with more in the works.

After navigating an empty nest, divorce, and fourteen years of being alone, Janet found her greatest love story in the winter of her life. She and her husband, Chuck, live in Indiana, where they spend mornings sipping coffee and watching the birds at their feeders. Janet is a proud mom, mother-in-love, grandmother, and Gaga to her precious great-grandchildren who keep her young.

When she's not writing, you'll find Janet teaching, speaking, or simply sitting a spell with friends who need encouragement. She believes in the power of gentle words, quiet love, and slathering grace over everyone you meet.

Connect with Janet at www.janethartleonard.com.

Also by Janet Hart Leonard

In *When the Hart Speaks: Whimsy and Wisdom from the Little House on the Alley*, Janet shares her moving story of finding God not in the church pew, but in the mud and mire of betrayal, grief, and disappointment. Through personal stories and heartfelt honesty, she shows how Faith emerges strongest in our darkest hours and how God writes a better story than we ever could if we trust Him with our pen. Perfect for anyone walking through unexpected heartache, this memoir offers hope when life looks nothing like you planned and assurance that God is working even in the unfair seasons. Discover how God can create beautiful purpose out of pain and give you more than you ever thought possible.

Thank you!

If you have been encouraged by this book, will you please leave a review on Amazon. Your review helps this book reach more readers than you might imagine.

Acknowledgements

There is no way to truly thank my **husband, Chuck,** for all his encouragement. I sometimes wonder what I've done to deserve someone as wonderful as he is. He never seems to grow tired of me or my words. I can't help but wipe away tears each time I read his foreword. His words hug my heart. Chuck Leonard, you are truly the love of my life.

I write a lot about my **mother**. I hope Heaven has a veil that lets her peek through and see everything I write about her. No child was ever loved more than I was. She and my dad were truly good people. I hope I have made them proud.

I love being a mom, mother-in-love, grandma, and now a Gaga. I love the bonus family I gained by marrying Chuck. I love you all. Thank you for giving me lots to write about.

A big thank you to my **daughter, Emily**, who contributed her chapter to this book. I think she may someday become a writer as well.

Thank you to **Andrea Lende** and **Ruth Hovsepian** at Beatitudes Publishing for giving my words a beautiful package. Your patience and guidance made a nervous second-time author feel less anxious.

To my bestie, **Patrice Lyttle**, you have held my hand and my heart for fifty-eight years. We are truly Lucy and Ethel. Life has been sweeter with you as my best friend.

To my **Tribe of Five, Patrice, Kathy, Linda, Joan,** and **Corinne**, you all have loved me well and kept me in line over the years. I know it's not always easy to do so.

To my writer communities, **Writer Chicks, Word Warriors, Hope Writers, and First Daughters,** your support and encouragement have kept me believing my words matter. Thank you for your inspiration and for showing me that pens and keyboards really can change the world.

To my fourth-grade teacher, **Marianne Jacobi,** who taught me that reading a great book would leave me wanting more.

To **my readers**, thank you for reading my words and telling me they matter.

www.ingramcontent.com/pod-product-compliance
Lightning Source LLC
Chambersburg PA
CBHW071756150726
47998CB00005B/1963